'By Road' - Across the Sea
The History of Atlantic Steam Navigation Company Ltd.

PUBLISHED BY

FERRY
Publications

Ferry Publications, 12 Millfields Close, Pentlepoir,
Kilgetty, Dyfed, Wales

ISBN 1 871947 07 3

Foreword

I t started with a fleet of tank landing ships surplus to requirements at the end of 1945, together with the thousands of military vehicles on the Continent needing to be returned to the U.K.

Colonel Frank Bustard was an entrepreneur. Working for White Star Line in the 'Thirties he formed Atlantic Steam Navigation Company with the idea of taking on the giants of the trans-Atlantic trade with a no frills service, an idea which was to be copied many years later in the airline industry. The Second World War forced him to shelve his plans, and his wartime experiences led to a re-think of the possibilities for his new Company.

Chartering three LSTs from the MOD, the pioneering Colonel launched the first ever ro-ro service for road vehicles and won a contract to return military cargo from Hamburg to Tilbury which was to operate until 1955. The rest of the story is history, the history which this book seeks to record.

It is a story which rightly emphasises that not only was A.S.N. the first shipping company to realise the potential of roll-on roll-off vessels, but also had the courage and foresight to develop this concept for the carriage of commercial goods which completely revolutionised international delivery methods.

Awaiting my call-up for National Service, I joined the Company in 1956 as a stop-gap. A.S.N. had by then become part of the nationalised British Transport Commission operating from Preston to Northern Ireland and from Tilbury to Antwerp still using the faithful fleet of LSTs. 1956 is a memorable year in the Company's history, not because I joined but because the entire fleet was requisitioned for use in the Suez conflict just at the time when plans were being formulated to expand.

When the vessels were returned the difficulties of trying to sell our new service to customers seemed almost insuperable as there were very few established national hauliers who were prepared to venture across the North Sea. A network of agents was appointed both in the U.K. and in Europe to make contact with the shippers, forwarders and manufacturers to introduce this new concept. A.S.N. were instrumental in creating the impetus for the waiving of restrictions in

Mr. John Palmer, Managing Director, P&O European Ferries, Felixstowe

Customs, fiscal and other matters which at the time impaired the development of international road haulage.

We also had to contend with opposition from existing general cargo shipping lines and port authorities, most of whom were content with the comfort of old-fashioned rate structures and established trade conferences. Despite this opposition, the simplicity of our service, together with the attendant savings in time and cost, were strong marketing weapons.

In operational terms, the outstanding success of early innovations is proven by the fact that many of our methods are still in use today throughout the industry — the only real difference being the greater size of ships and the increased length and weight of the vehicles carried.

The Company itself has, over the years, undergone many changes and has now been taken over on three occasions since originally formed. The industry has changed quite dramatically, particularly in recent years, and although justifiably proud of the past we must constantly prepare for the future.

The greatest possible tribute that can be paid to any pioneer is for history to record success. The contribution A.S.N. has made to the development of commercial ro-ro has been immense and the effect of this revolution was to bring a fundamental change in the development of British trade.

There will, no doubt, be more changes to come, and I am sure that, with the strength of the P&O Group behind us, we can have every confidence in the future.

John Palmer, Managing Director,
P&O European Ferries (Felixstowe) Ltd.

*The **Gaelic Ferry** inward to Tilbury in 1965. (Fotoflite F/32)*

ONE

The A.S.N. Years

The founder and major driving force of the Atlantic Steam Navigation Co. Ltd, Frank Bustard, was born in Liverpool on 20th February 1886. On leaving school at the age of 16, he joined the then White Star Line as the last of the company's office apprentices. As a postage clerk he earned 5/- (25p) a week working 13 hours a day. Later, at the age of 21, he was appointed as the Chief Assistant to the Passenger Department Manager (Second and Third Class steerage).

By 1934, Frank Bustard was the Passenger Traffic Manager. In the same year, the Government merged Cunard Line with White Star Line. He was asked by the Directors of both companies to accept service with the new merged operation, but he declined, as he felt that his old company would soon be entirely submerged and Cunard would become the prominent operating name. How right he was!

Frank Bustard felt that Cunard would be entirely opposed to his ideas for broadening the approach to travel on the Northern Atlantic with cheaper fares. He felt now was the right time for cheaper fares, to offer more opportunities for people to travel on the Atlantic. He planned to offer a one-way fare of £10 on his new service, with à la carte menus as an extra, similar to some of the Atlantic air services developed in the 'Eighties.

He left Oceanic House and opened his own office in Norway House, right opposite the old White Star Offices. He employed three ex-White Star Line employees who were prepared to come in with him. Two years later the Atlantic Steam Navigation Company Limited was formed. A new North Atlantic shipping company was frowned upon by the Government of the day, since it would mean competition for the newly-formed Cunard White Star Line.

Following the formation of the Company, he set about negotiating the acquisition of the necessary vessels to operate his new service. Frank Bustard tendered to purchase the vessels of the Red Star Line which had been put up for sale as part of the I.M.F.'s budgetary measures following the Depression of the early 'Thirties. The ships offered for sale included the **Belgenland, Pennland, Westernland, Minnetonka** and the **Minnewaska**.

Frank Bustard was not successful in securing the vessels he planned to purchase. In view of this outcome, he decided to have designs prepared for two liners for his Atlantic service, and he approached Vickers Armstrong. The two

Lt. Col. Frank Bustard, the founder of A.S.N.

liners were designed to carry 1,500 passengers in two classes (Cabin and Tourist). Two very attractive three-funnelled ships of about 33,000 gross tons were designed, with a service speed of 22 knots.

By late 1936 it was rumoured that the new vessels were to be named **Silverswift** and **Silverfalcon.** With a contract price of £2.25 million per vessel and tentative delivery dates agreed, A.S.N. proposed sailings from Liverpool to New York via Dun Laoghaire every 10 days. The project was complete.

In October 1938, Frank Bustard approached the Bank of England for financial assistance but, due to the negative attitude of the Government of the day, his request for a loan of £2.5 million was turned down.

Frank Bustard pursued his project nevertheless with undaunted determination, even approaching the established shipping companies Orient and Anchor Lines with his plans. Events in Europe were to overtake the new Company's plans, with the Munich crisis and finally the outbreak of the Second World War in 1939.

Frank Bustard was called up for the Army Reserve. During the War he made friends with Don Smith, of Messrs Smith,

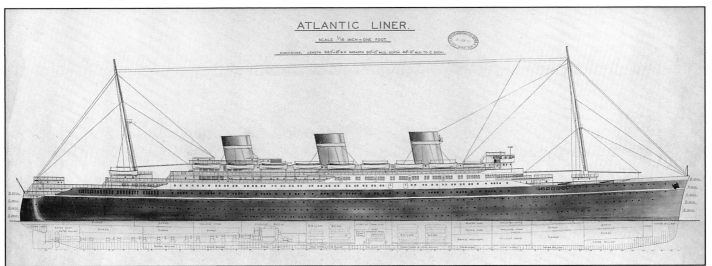

The Vickers Armstrong design for the Atlantic Steam Navigation Company's liners.

Coggins and Company, the leading stevedores in Liverpool for the Government shipments to the Forces overseas. Both Frank Bustard and Don Smith were present at the trials of the Naval LSTs for discharging military vehicles over their bow ramps onto the sands at New Brighton and over the sloping quayside of Barrow Docks. They both considered at the time that there surely would be a commercial use for these craft after the War.

Following the end of the Second World War, Frank Bustard opened his office at his War damaged home in Dulwich. In a short period of time, he managed to get office premises in the French Line House in Cockspur Street and there he was to remain until he transferred to Craig Court House in Whitehall.

Frank Bustard tried to revive his North Atlantic plans, but it soon became clear to him that no suitable ships were available and building new tonnage was out of the question.

His thoughts then went back to his meeting with Don Smith during the War, regarding operating LSTs for commercial use. He opened negotiations for the charter of three LSTs with the Ministry of War Transport, the Admiralty and the War Office. Following protracted talks, he was successful in chartering for three years three British LSTs, 3519, 3534 and 3512. They were to be named **Empire Baltic**, **Empire Cedric** and **Empire Celtic**, thus perpetuating the names of White Star vessels.

The chartered vessels had to be adapted for their new role. First the accommodation on board had to be improved and alterations in the engine room and boiler room had also to be made. Modified funnels and navigational aids had also to be provided before they could enter service.

The outstanding feature of the LSTs was, of course, the device by which vehicles were loaded and discharged. Two doors opened outwards from the bow, and from within a watertight ramp was lowered across which the vehicles were driven. The capacity of the LSTs on two decks was 12 tanks and about 60 to 80 lorries of the day, or about 200 cars. The vessels had two 15 ton derricks immediately forward of the bridge for lifting cargo on and off the quay. The speed of the 'Empire' Class vessels was 10 knots.

To make the initial enterprise work, the Board of Directors was strengthened. The Board had already Mr S.R. Hogg, an eminent City Accountant who had stood by the Company during the War period. Mr Don Smith then joined, to be followed by Major General Szlumper, who had been involved before the War with the Southern Railway and during the War as Director of Transportation. These three Directors and their personal friends provided the necessary capital to get the show started and develop the Transport Ferry Service, as it was later to become known.

As far as the command of the vessels was concerned, the Company worked on the principle of employing Masters with practical and R.N.R. experience.

On 11th September 1946, the first voyage of the Atlantic Steam Navigation Co. Ltd (A.S.N.) took place, when the **Empire Baltic** sailed from Tilbury to Rotterdam with a full cargo of 64 vehicles for the Dutch Government. The first voyage is richly illustrated by Michael Bustard in the Company's "Log Book" in 1971:-

"Our cargo in the tank deck consisted of new vehicles for the Dutch Army and, although they were all runners, the loading, under the supervision of "Barney" French, took several hours of the preceding day. Under the command of Captain J. W. Rennie, we finally left the old 26 Berth at Tilbury at 11 a.m. on that Wednesday morning twenty-five years ago. The voyage to Rotterdam in those days was good for 24 hours and we did not pass the Hook of Holland until early the following morning, finally arriving at our "berth", nothing

*Two views of the first LST's to be chartered to the Company in 1946, (top) the **Empire Cedric** and the **Empire Celtic** (pictured above). (Foto Flite Library)*

more than a deserted sandy beach near the Waalhaven, at 10 a.m. There was no quay alongside, no shore hard, just nothing - the ship being held by the stern anchor. Before the ramp could be lowered, the two bow doors had to be opened and before they could be opened the beams holding them together had to be unbolted and removed. This process took at least an hour, with a new and untrained crew.

Eventually, the bow doors slowly opened, only to find that the bottom corners of the port door stuck in the sandy bottom of the beach. The hero of the day - a Mr. Bottomley of Messrs. Smith, Coggins, our stevedores - called for a spade and jumping into the water fully clothed immediately began to shovel sand away some 4' below the surface of the water. Eventually the door freed itself, thanks, I suspect, more to the tipping of the ship than to his digging efforts; the bow ramp came down and the cargo of lorries was driven ashore -getting rather wet in the process. The whole operation took place in this rather desolate section of the Port of Rotterdam against a skyline of heavily blitzed warehouses, and I well remember the only spectators of this historic occasion were some rather thin and hungry looking Dutch boys leaning on the handle-bars of their bicycles.

Although the operation of discharge was complete by lunch-time, there was no question of any speedy return to Tilbury and orders were given for the ship to sail again at 8 a.m. the following morning. The first few voyages of the Company's ships followed this rather leisurely pattern of operation and any attempts to speed up the process were usually demolished by vague - but no less ominous - references to the need for an overnight examination of the boilers.

Our protracted stay in Rotterdam enabled Captain Rennie and myself to accept the Agent's invitation to join him and his wife ashore that evening. After the rigours of the outward voyage, we found little difficulty in persuading ourselves to accept. And what rigours they were in those days, especially for the luckless passenger! The only room in the ship available to passengers was the Saloon, where one had to sit, read, talk, eat or drink for the entire voyage - this could be quite a feat of endurance especially if one were to suffer bad weather on the 48-hour passage to Hamburg. In those days the three meals of the day were rather compressed in their time span, breakfast being at 8 a.m., lunch at 12 noon and the last meal of the day, high tea, at 5 p.m.!

After high tea (which consisted of one main course, such as cold meat, invariably followed by bread and jam), the one passenger table in the saloon was cleared away and there was nothing left to do but to sit in the same place. The only diversions were conversation, playing cards, chess and cribbage. There was no separate lounge for the officers then and they occupied the starboard table of the saloon, whilst the Master, Chief Engineer and passengers occupied the port table. This was rather a long table, which meant that if one were seated on the left-hand side of the Master on the bulkhead side, one could be "imprisoned" for what seemed on occasions a very long meal-time by four or five other passengers, who all had to slide along the shiny leather bench-seat in order to allow one out. One could, of course, have asked the Master to move from his seat, but such a request was unthinkable.

Other rigours suffered in the early days included the complete absence of any plumbing in the cabins. Passengers shared the Officers' bathroom, where three washbasins and the one bath were all in the same room - the bath being discreetly, but ineffectively, screened off by a green canvas curtain. For passengers, however the most fearsome trial of all was the dreaded "outside" cabins, to which access could only be gained by going outside onto the dark and open Upper Deck, dodging the rain as best one could. Once in there for the night, access to the more convenient parts of the ship was difficult, if not impossible, without the exasperation of getting fully dressed again.

*An interior view looking aft on the main vehicle deck of the **Empire Gaelic**. (John Jolly personal collection)*

Captain Rennie and I were duly picked up by the Agent and his wife, who conducted us to a rather decorous club situated in the middle of the park in Rotterdam. Entertainment was provided by a lady clothed entirely in black who tinkled away at an enormous grand piano -also in black. For some unaccountable reason, it had been presumed by the Agent that we had already partaken of our evening meal. Unfortunately, we had not. The agony of this misunderstanding was only relieved at about 10 p.m. by the appearance of a few beautiful - but rather thinly-cut sandwiches. The liquid refreshment consisted solely of small glasses of Dutch gin, which on top of our rather empty stomachs had a chloroform-like effect on our eyelids.

The next morning we left Rotterdam at 8 a.m. and finally reached Tilbury on the morning of the fourth day. Our odyssey had taken three days, had been accomplished without radar or Decca Navigator, we had received

*Two of Pilkington Brothers' glass lorries on board the **Empire Cedric**. (P&O Library collection)*

No. 1 Berth and the original linkspan at Preston.
(Author's collection)

The **Empire Gaelic** approaching Douglas Harbour with a new consignment of buses for the Isle of Man. (John Jolly personal collection)

compulsorily the assistance of twelve different pilots - but it had been a success and it was, after all, the *first* of a very considerable number."

Part of Chipperfield's Circus being taken on board the **Empire Celtic**. (John Jolly personal collection)

Empire Nordic. (John Jolly personal collection)

Following the Rotterdam maiden voyage of A.S.N., the Company then used their new vessels to ferry backwards and forwards thousands of vehicles for the Army from Tilbury to Hamburg. This service was later moved to Antwerp in 1955. The original trio of LSTs was joined by a further vessel of similar class in 1948, the **Empire Doric,** following the Company being able to convince commercial operators to support a new service between mainland Britain and Ulster.

A.S.N. had originally wanted to open their new service to Northern Ireland from Liverpool, but there was opposition from other operators at the Mersey port. In the light of Liverpool turning away A.S.N., the Company decided to establish themselves at Preston in Lancashire, On the other hand the port authorities at the Antrim port of Larne were to welcome the new route.

Special port facilities had to be built both at Preston and Larne before the service could start. At Larne, end-loading facilities were available in the form of a ramp built by the Army during the War. At Preston a new terminal and ramp had to be built. A pontoon from the Mulberry Harbour was used for the ramp. The floating pontoon was connected to the quay via a bridge. Mr J. F. Jolly recalls the development of the Preston service and the first sailing:-

"What a start, I will never forget it, in fact I can still smell it! The best the Preston Port Authority was prepared to offer us by way of an Administration Block was one small partitioned-off portion of the then cattle lairage, the floor of which was covered with straw and you know what! The din was deafening, the pong was worse and Doreen Rowles, my typist, was terrified - she had an allergy about bulls. I can remember dictating a letter to her amidst strong odours and loud bellowing of cattle.

Shore staff at Preston at this time included Mr. John Jolly, Mr. Frank Napoleon, Miss Doreen Rowles and the late Captain W. S. Thornton. Larne had rather a chequered period at this time, the first Traffic Superintendent being a young man named Carroll from London Office followed by Mr. Jordan, and subsequently Ian Duffin.

The first cargo carried comprised 14 items and two lorries each carrying 65 gas cookers which were shipped on this voyage on behalf of Messrs. Moffats of Blackburn must logically have been the first two commerical vehicles in the world to have been carried in this manner as freight.

At this stage we were looked upon as "Adventurers" and not "Venturers" by the Port Authorities and the shipping fraternity gave us only six months to live. Shortly after the commencement of the Irish Service we obtained a contract to carry some 200 pre-fabricated houses, loose, like a pack of cards, on trailers for erection in Larne. One of our

*Captain H.T. Green with the Preston pilot on the **Empire Gaelic**.*

original and most interesting cargoes in the early days was the carrying of Messrs. Pilkington lorries loaded with sheet glass which again was the first time that glass had been carried in this manner by sea. This became a most valuable selling point to us, for in over twelve months we never cracked a single pane whereas by the conventional method of shipping their breakages had averaged 25% per annum.

The first circus we carried was from Larne to Preston, a small Irish company named Sandow's Circus."

Following the inaugural sailing on 21st May 1948, the **Empire Cedric** maintained the Northern Ireland service, initially offering two sailings a week.

When the Larne service opened, sceptics declared that it would not last more than six months and in any case would only attract capital goods of high value - how wrong they were to be!

The early days of the Northern Ireland service are recorded by Captain H. T. Green who joined the Company in 1947:-

"I spent some months with A.S.N. on the **Empire Baltic**, on the Tilbury-Hamburg service, being then transferred to the **Empire Cedric** (Captain Johnson) just prior to her sailing for Belfast via Southampton where we picked up the pontoon for the Preston terminal.

From Southampton we proceeded to Birkenhead where the pontoon was discharged and there I first met Captain Thornton who proved to be a tower of strength over the years.

After spending some weeks at Belfast converting the ship

for carrying drivers we proceeded to Preston to inaugurate the Preston-Northern Ireland service which commenced late in May 1948, It is interesting to note **Empire Cedric** was the first of our vessels to hold a Passenger Certificate, the number permitted being 50.

Pioneering the Roll-on/Roll-off service at Preston - the first of its kind in the world - gave one a great deal of satisfaction and many heartaches. We had to learn and learn fast. Apart from trouble with the pontoon at Preston which, being water ballasted and not sub-divided, tipped which-ever way the water ran, our first arrival at Larne was somewhat of a fiasco. Crowds on the quay, the "red carpet" treatment -to find the shore linkspan would not connect but by dint of rapid work on the part of a burner, the offending parts were cut away and all was well. Our faces were a bit red at the time but it was our first introduction to Davey Logan (the Manager of Larne Harbour) who was a master of improvisation. I recall in the initial stages I had to do all the driving as the dockers were totally inexperienced and having observed the peculiarities of the pontoon were somewhat nervous.

Some two months after starting the service I got my first command in the Company relieving Captain Johnson. I have never quite forgiven him for leaving a cricket ball in a drawer under the bunk which was locked; as the furniture in the LSTs was made of metal the effect when the vessel was rolling can well be imagined. I still claim I did not have a wink of sleep for the whole time he was away.

Immediately after this I went to Govan to stand by the refit of the **Empire Doric** and subsequently took command of her followed by the **Empire Gaelic**. Later I had a repeat performance as regards the **Empire Cymric**."

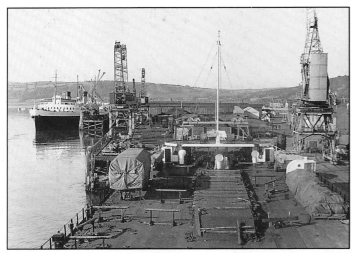

*Looking forward from the **Empire Cedric** at Larne Harbour in the Fifties. The railway vessel, the **Hampton Ferry**, can be seen pending her morning departure to Stranraer. (John Jolly personal collection)*

A splendid looking lorry of The Bentley Tileries Ltd. Group on board one of the early LSTs of the Company. (P&O Library collection)

Prior to the opening of the service, The Transport Ferry Service as it was to become known for marketing, had a fleet of five vessels and managed a further seven ships for the War Department in the Middle East and Far East.

Trading continued to expand on the Preston - Larne service and in 1950 services were extended from the Lancashire port to include Belfast. A further vessel, the **Empire Gaelic**, joined the ranks of the fleet to open the new service. The Belfast link opened in 1950 and sailings from Preston were soon to be increased to between six and seven a week to either Larne or Belfast.

In April 1954, A.S.N. was taken over by the British Transport Commission (BTC) as part of the Labour Government's policy for nationalisation. There was to be little change in operations of the Company at first.

The next year saw a further three LSTs being chartered into the fleet, the **Empire Cymric**, **Empire Doric** and **Empire Nordic**.

With the Hamburg service terminated in 1955, a new service to Antwerp was started from Tilbury. The fleet of seven ships was to be split with the usual three ships based at Tilbury and the other LSTs on the Preston services to Northern Ireland.

During late 1956, the Government took over the entire fleet of A.S.N., for use in the Mediterranean in the Suez Crisis. Preparations and the Company's involvement in the Suez Crisis are dealt with later in this book.

It was not until January 1957 that the drive-on services were re-established at the end of hostilities. During the Suez War the Preston unit-load service was maintained by chartering three British coasters for nearly a month, and four German-registered ships for the rest of the Suez War.

A.S.N. were made responsible for the management of 12 Admiralty LST's brought out of lay-up during the crisis. Bird names were chosen for the managed ships; **Empire Curlew, Empire Fulmar, Empire Gannet, Empire Grebe, Empire Guillemot, Empire Gull, Empire Kittiwake, Empire**

*Not an inch to spare. A packed **Empire Cedric** moves out of Preston Harbour into the River Ribble. (Captain H.T. Green, Retired, collection)*

8

Empire Doric. (Foto Flite 14923)

Petrel, Empire Puffin, Empire Skua, Empire Tern and the **Empire Shearwater.** A.S.N. were already managing for the War Department their fleet of LSTs namely **Charles MacLeod, Evan Gibb, Frederick Clover, Humphrey Gale, Maxwell Brander, Reginald Kerr** and **Snowden Smith.**

This large fleet of 26 LSTs was all in A.S.N. colours. At the time 30 ships were managed and operated by the Atlantic Steam Navigation Company.

Subsequently one of the 'Seabird' class ships, the **Empire Shearwater**, did see commercial service during 1959, when she was chartered from the Government by Townsend Brothers Car Ferries Limited for service between Dover and Calais. Sadly the pioneering company was to find the charter of this LST unsuccessful.

A.S.N. was later to hand over the management of the War Department LST fleet of 7 vessels to the British India Steam Navigation Company Limited. On transfer to the new management, the vessels were given new colours.

During 1957, A.S.N. were to acquire their first two purpose-built vessels with the financial backing of the BTC. The new vessels were especially designed for the Company for the carriage of lorries, trailers, cars and passengers.

The first vessel, the **Bardic Ferry**, was launched on a rather dull day on the 5th March 1957, at the renowned yard of William Denny and Brothers at Dumbarton.

The design of the new ships was developed from the 11 years of operation of LSTs, and also took account of M.O.D. specification in case either vessel had to be called for military service. The **Bardic Ferry** and her later sister the **Ionic Ferry,** were designed to take up to 70 vehicles or trailers on the vehicle deck, reached by a stern ramp. The main car decks of both ships were strengthened to carry tanks in the light of the M.O.D. requirements. The headroom in the new vessels allowed sufficient height for a double decker bus to be carried on board. On the other deck 20 containers could be accommodated, loaded by either dockside cranes or the ship's own 20-ton electric crane aft.

The **Empire Gaelic** arrives at Larne on 10th May 1956, at the opening of the Phoenix Quay. (John Jolly personal collection)

Empire Curlew. (A. Morehen collection)

9

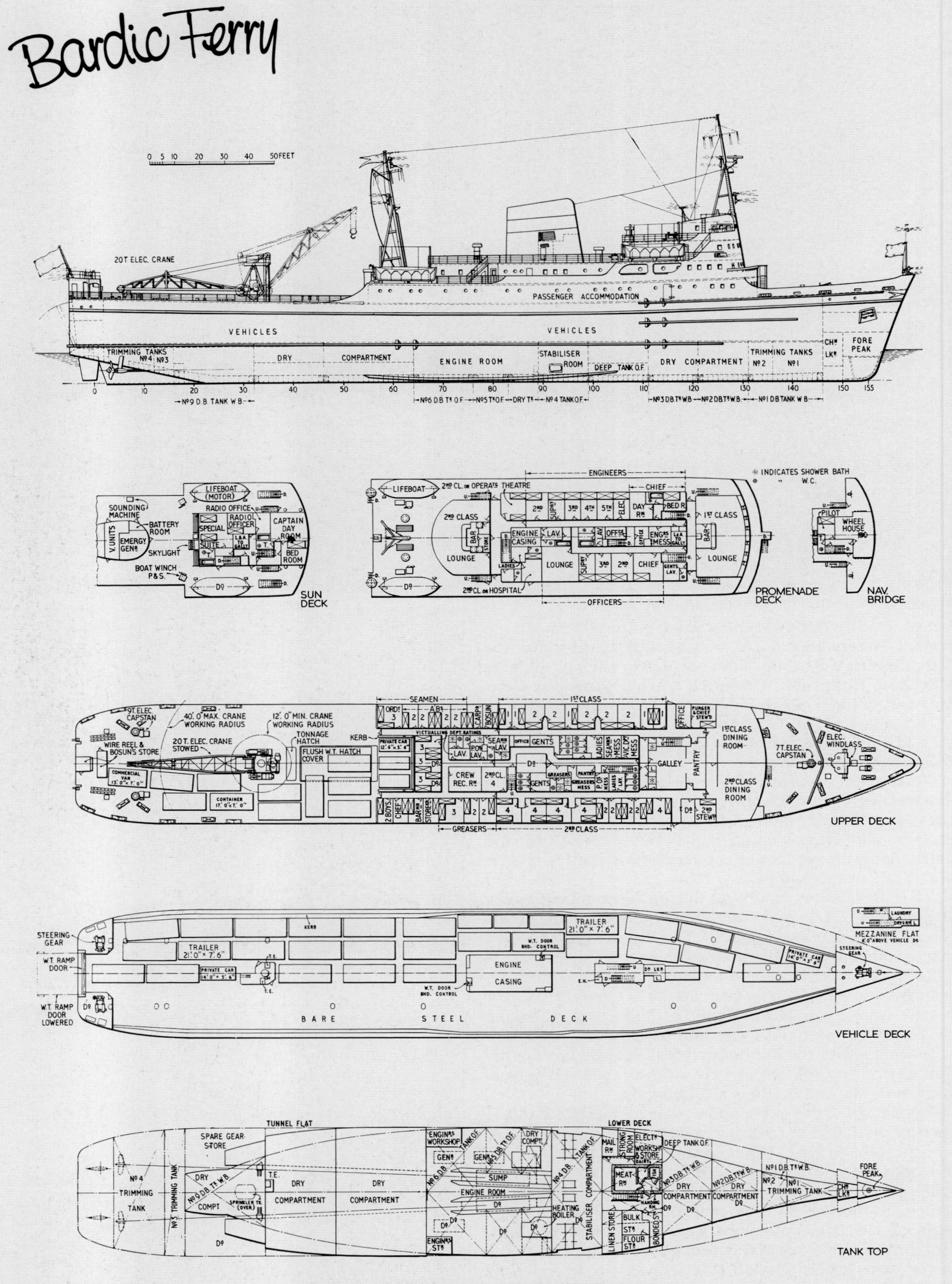

Bardic Ferry

Sun Deck (top profile — starboard elevation)

0 5 10 20 30 40 50FEET

20T. ELEC. CRANE

PASSENGER ACCOMMODATION

VEHICLES   VEHICLES

FORE PEAK   CH⁺ LK⁺

TRIMMING TANKS Nº4 Nº3 | DRY COMPARTMENT | ENGINE ROOM | STABILISER ROOM | DEEP TANK O.F. | DRY COMPARTMENT | TRIMMING TANKS Nº2 Nº1

→ Nº9 D.B. TANK W.B. ←

Nº6 D.B. Tᵏˢ O.F.   Nº5 Tᵏ O.F.   DRY Tᵏ   Nº4 TANK O.F.   Nº3 D.B Tᵏ W.B.   Nº2 D.B Tᵏ W.B.   Nº1 D.B TANK W.B.

0   10   20   30   40   50   60   70   80   90   100   110   120   130   140   150 155

SUN DECK

SOUNDING MACHINE — V. UNITS — BATTERY ROOM — EMERG⁺ GEN⁺ — SKYLIGHT — BOAT WINCH P.& S. — LIFEBOAT (MOTOR) — RADIO OFFICE — RADIO OFFICER — SPECIAL SUITE — CAPTAIN DAY ROOM — BED ROOM

PROMENADE DECK

* INDICATES SHOWER BATH W.C.

LIFEBOAT — 2ᴺᴰ CL. or OPERAᵗˢ THEATRE — ENGINEERS — CHIEF — 2ᴺᴰ SUPᵗ 3ᴿᴰ 4ᵀᴴ 5ᵀᴴ ELEC. DAY R⁺ BED R⁺ — 2ᴺᴰ CLASS LOUNGE — BAR STORE — ENGINE CASING — LAV. — OFFEᵗ — ENGⁱ⁺ MESS — 1ˢᵀ CLASS — LADIES — LOUNGE — SUP⁺ 3ᴿᴰ 2ᴺᴰ — CHIEF — GENTS. LAV. — BAR — LOUNGE — OFFICERS — 2ᴺᴰ CL. or HOSPITAL

NAV. BRIDGE

PILOT — WHEEL HOUSE

UPPER DECK

9T. ELEC. CAPSTAN — 40'. 0" MAX. CRANE WORKING RADIUS — 20 T. ELEC. CRANE STOWED — 12'. 0" MIN. CRANE WORKING RADIUS — TONNAGE HATCH — FLUSH W.T. HATCH COVER — KERB — WIRE REEL & BOSUN'S STORE — COMMERCIAL VAN 15' 0" × 7' 0" — CONTAINER 17' 0" × 7' 0"

SEAMEN — 1ˢᵀ CLASS — ORDⁱ AB'S CARPⁱ BOSUN — OFFICE — PURSER ⁱCHIEF ⁱ STEW⁺ — 1ˢᵀ CLASS DINING ROOM — 7T. ELEC. CAPSTAN — ELEC. WINDLASS — VICTUALLING DEPT RATINGS — PRIVATE CAR 14' 6" × 5' 6" — SEAMⁱ LAV. — OFFICE — GENTS — LADIES — SEAMⁱ MESS — P.O. MESS — GALLEY — PANTRY — 2ᴺᴰ CLASS DINING ROOM — CREW REC. Rᴹ — 2ᴺᴰ CL. — GENTS — GREASERS — PANTRY — GREASERS MESS — P.O. LAV. — 2 BOYS — CHEFS — BARᴹ STORES — GREASERS — 2ᴺᴰ CLASS — 2ᴺᴰ STEW⁺

VEHICLE DECK

STEERING GEAR — W.T. RAMP DOOR — W.T. RAMP DOOR LOWERED — TRAILER 21'. 0" × 7'. 6" — KERB — PRIVATE CAR 14' 0" × 5' 6" — W.T. DOOR BHD. CONTROL — ENGINE CASING — PRIVATE CAR 14' 0" × 5' 6" — LAUNDRY — DRYⁱⁿ⁺ — MEZZANINE FLAT 6' 0" ABOVE VEHICLE Dᴷ — STEERING GEAR

BARE   STEEL   DECK

TANK TOP (Lower Deck)

TUNNEL FLAT — SPARE GEAR STORE — Nº4 TRIMMING TANK — Nº3 TRIMMING TANK — Nº9 D.B. Tᵏ W.B — DRY COMPT. — SPRINKLER Tᵏ (OVER) — DRY COMPARTMENT — DRY COMPARTMENT — ENGINⁱ⁺ WORKSHOP — GENⁱ — Nº6 D.B. — GENⁱ⁺ D.B. Tᵏ O.F. — SUMP — ENGINE ROOM — HEATING BOILER — ENGINⁱ⁺ Sᵗ⁺ — DRY TANK O.F. — DRY COMPT. — Nº4 D.B. TANK O.F. — STABILISER COMPARTMENT — LINEN STORE — FLOUR Sᵗ⁺ — BONDED Sᵗ⁺ — BULK⁺ — HARDⁱⁿ⁺ ROOM — MEAT Rᴹ — STRONG ROOM — ELECᵗ WORKSHOP & STORE — MAIL Rᴹ — DEEP TANK O.F. — Nº3 D.B Tᵏ W.B — Nº2 D.B Tᵏ W.B — DRY COMPARTMENT — DRY COMPARTMENT — Nº2 TRIMMING TANK — Nº1 — FORE PEAK — CH⁺ LK⁺

LOWER DECK

General arrangement drawings of the Bardic Ferry built by William Denny and Brothers, Dumbarton

Bardic Ferry

1. The **Bardic Ferry** on trials in the Clyde during August 1957.
2. Sun Deck
3. Second Class Lounge

4. First Class Dining Room

5. First Class Lounge Bar
6. First Class Cabin De-Luxe
(All photographs author's collection)

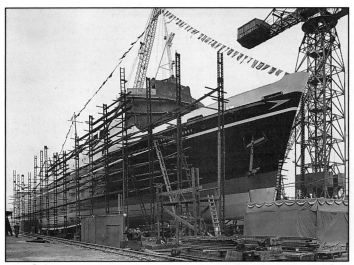

The Bardic Ferry (Ship No. 1489) on the stocks prior to her launch. (H. Irwin collection)

Vauxhall cars and Bedford vans being loaded on the Empire Baltic at Tilbury. (P&O Library collection)

Accommodation was provided for 55 passengers in two classes. A two-berth special suite cabin, attractively furnished and equipped with its own bathroom, was situated on the sun deck forward. Accommodation was also provided for a further 15 First Class passengers on the upper deck in five single-berth and five double-berth cabins. Accommodation was provided on the upper and promenade decks for 38 Second Class passengers in five double-berth cabins and seven 4-berth cabins.

Both First and Second Class passengers had their own dining room and lounge facilities. Both classes of ship were fitted with Denny Brown stabilisers, to provide the maximum comfort for passengers and for the protection of the cargo on board.

The Captain's suite, day room, bedroom and separate toilet were situated on the sun deck, while the engineer and deck officers' cabins were on the promenade deck. A separate recreation room and mess rooms were provided for the crew and a separate lounge for officers was located on the promenade deck adjacent to their cabin accommodation.

The **Bardic Ferry** made her maiden voyage on 2nd September 1957 between Preston and Larne under the command of Captain Green. The 'Bardic's' sister was launched in May 1958 and entered service from Preston on 10th October.

Following the **Ionic Ferry** entering service on the Northern Irish service, the **Bardic Ferry** was transferred to the Antwerp link from Tilbury.

The Belfast link continued to be maintained by one of the LSTs with the occasional stand-in by the **Ionic Ferry**

During late 1959, the first LST, **Empire Cedric,** was withdrawn from service. In the same year the Company unveiled plans to build two further vessels based on the design of the **Bardic Ferry**. The two new ships were ordered from Ailsa Shipbuilding Company Limited, Troon and were to be of a very similar design and appearance to the 'Bardic' and 'Ionic', but were to be slightly larger than the twins first built.

The two new vessels could accommodate about 50 lorries and trailers on the main deck with a headroom of 4.4 metres

The Bardic Ferry is manoeuvred to her fitting-out basin, following her launch on 5th March 1957. (Captain H.T. Green, Retired, collection)

12

*Sisters together at Preston. The **Ionic Ferry**, pictured left, is dressed overall prior to her maiden voyage and the **Bardic Ferry** can be seen prior to her departure to Tilbury to take up the European services of A.S.N. (Captain H.T. Green, Retired, collection)*

It is interesting to note that the **Nordic Ferry**, currently operating for P&O European Ferries on the Felixstowe - Zeebrugge route, has a headroom of 5 metres. On the upper deck there was space for some 30 containers, handled by a 20-ton deck crane. The new vessels were built as one class ships with accommodation for 35 passengers in two berth cabins-de-luxe on the promenade deck and two and four berth cabins on the upper deck. Both new ships had an impressive dining room and lounge bar, with separate club room facilities for lorry drivers on board.

The first of the new vessels, named **Cerdic Ferry**, was launched on 16th February 1961 and entered service during November the same year. The **Cerdic Ferry** initially operated one trip a week to Rotterdam and two sailings to Antwerp. On the entry into service of the **Cerdic Ferry**, the

*Captain H.T. Green and his officers on board the **Ionic Ferry** at Preston. From right to left, Alec Holden — Purser, Chief Officer Adamson, Captain Green, Chief Engineer Thomas and Norman Surplus — 2nd Engineer. (Captain H.T. Green, Retired, collection)*

Ionic Ferry was transferred back to the Preston - Northern Ireland services.

On the arrival of the **Cerdic Ferry's** sister, the **Doric Ferry** (launched on 27th October 1961) in April 1962, a daily service to the Continent became possible from Tilbury. The **Cerdic Ferry** for the most part maintained the Rotterdam service opened in 1960, and her sister was mostly employed on the link to Belgium.

During 1962 the British Transport Commission (BTC) was dissolved and A.S.N.'s ownership was transferred under the Transport Act of 1962 to the newly-formed Transport Holding Company.

*The **Ionic Ferry** pictured shortly after her launch. (Captain H.T. Green, Retired, collection)*

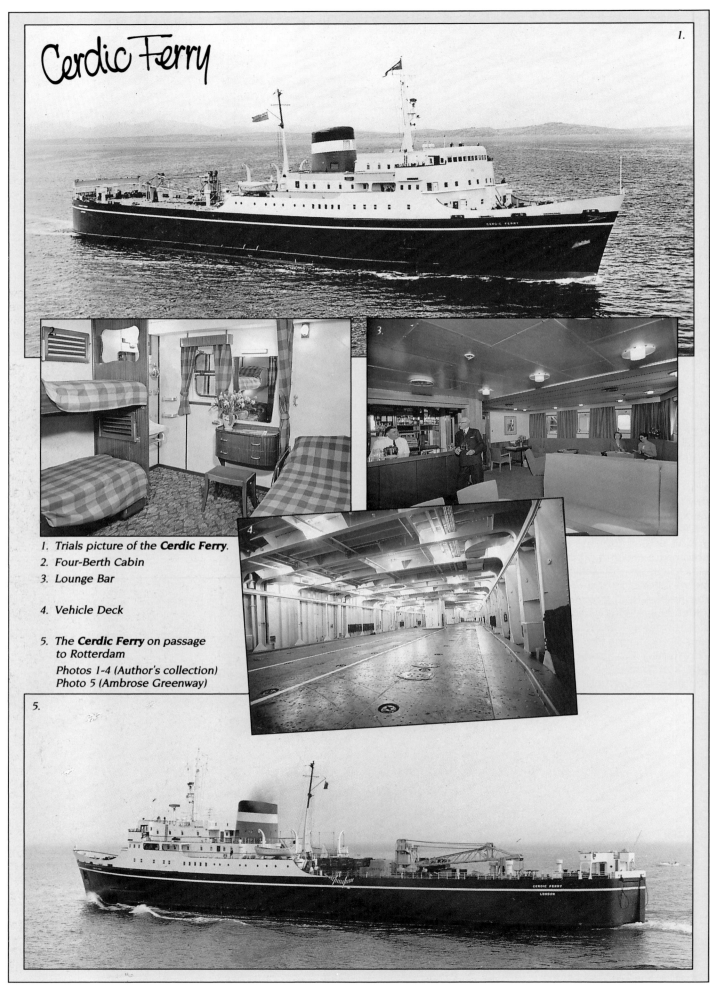

Cerdic Ferry

1. Trials picture of the **Cerdic Ferry**.
2. Four-Berth Cabin
3. Lounge Bar

4. Vehicle Deck

5. The **Cerdic Ferry** on passage
   to Rotterdam

   Photos 1-4 (Author's collection)
   Photo 5 (Ambrose Greenway)

*The **Ionic Ferry** on passage to Larne, following her entry into service in October 1957. (Foto Flite X 1104)*

With four purpose-built ships in operation, the LSTs were gradually withdrawn from operations. By 1963, only the **Empire Nordic** remained in service on the Preston -Belfast service. The **Empire Nordic** made some interesting trips during her career with the Atlantic Steam Navigation Company which are worthy of note. In August 1961 she sailed from Ardrossan to Antwerp with military stores and some three years later she made a one off trip between Preston and Dublin.

The **Empire Nordic** made her last sailing in December 1966, following the Company deciding it was too expensive to maintain her.

With the pressing demand for additional capacity in the fleet in the mid-'Sixties, A.S.N. purchased the **Pima Country**, a US Tank Landing Ship, in 1965. Following the purchase of this vessel, she was towed from Philadelphia to the Tyne yard of Smith's Dock Company Limited for alterations.

The new vessel, renamed **Baltic Ferry**, had no passenger accommodation and funnels had to be provided on the ship before she entered service! She could carry about 45 lorries

on her main deck and containers could be carried on her other deck. The vessel was only to have a short spell with the Company, until 1968.

In October 1963, the Company's fifth purpose-built vessel was launched. She was very similar to her predecessors in design. The new ship, the **Gaelic Ferry**, was built as a one class vessel with accommodation for 28 passengers. On her main cargo deck she could accommodate over 100 trailers or lorries. The **Gaelic Ferry** did not have her own crane on her upper deck, like her earlier sisters.

The **Gaelic Ferry** entered service at Tilbury initially, prior to the new terminal at Felixstowe being opened. Sailings on the Antwerp and Rotterdam services were now increased from six to eight sailings per week.

In March 1964, after the **Gaelic Ferry** had been in service for only a couple of weeks, news came that the vessel was to receive a Royal visit. Preparations for the memorable day in the Company's history are recorded by Keith Aston.

"It all began as a closely guarded secret. Only a select few knew anything about it, but some outward sign had to be made. For instance, the Continental sailing schedule, for some unknown reason, had its pattern altered for the week commencing 23rd March.

*The **Doric Ferry** captured against the sunlight. (Author's collection)*

*The **Baltic Ferry** on passage to Preston. (Foto Flite 66/2283)*

Prince Philip at Tilbury Docks during his visit to the port, pictured with Mr. F.B. Bolton, Chairman of A.S.N. and Mr. M.K. Bustard, Managing Director of the Company. (P&O Library collection)

*An aerial view of the A.S.N. Tilbury terminal, taken in the 'Sixties with **Doric Ferry** at the linkspan. (Foto Flite 66/1866)*

Rumour, otherwise known as the "grapevine", gave various reasons but, like most rumours, there was an element of truth. A visit was in the air, but who was the visitor? The Beatles? Mr. Marples (Minister of Transport)? You paid your money and you took your choice.

On Wednesday 4th March, a secret conclave was held in the Board Room at Head Office and the name of the visitor was divulged, but once again the name was not to be mentioned outside those four walls, until a certain publication gave the news officially,

Time passed. Rumour spread at Head Office, at Tilbury, and even as far away as Antwerp. Some guesses were accurate, but had to be denied without a nervous twitch or other sign that the guesses were correct. Other guesses were way off the mark. One of the boatmen at Tilbury told me, very confidentially, that the **Gaelic Ferry** was bringing over the Dutch Royal Family from Rotterdam. This information, which could neither be confirmed nor denied, covered the facts. The **Gaelic Ferry** was on the Rotterdam service that week. The crew were beginning an intensified programme of tidying up an otherwise immaculate ship. It all added up!

Captain J. W. Cowie, Master of the **Gaelic Ferry**, and the writer, who were amongst the select few who knew officially the name of the visitor, had to present poker faces when challenged by the "know-alls" who guessed accurately or otherwise.

A lot of preparation had to be undertaken at No. 4 Berth, Tilbury Dock. As the days rolled by, and the date of the visit approached, still without official authorisation to mention the visitor's name or the date of the visit, tension mounted. Some positive action had to be taken.

On Wednesday 18th March the Court Circular announcing the visit of His Royal Highness Prince Philip, Duke of Edinburgh to the m.v **Gaelic Ferry** on Tuesday 24th March at Tilbury was published.

The day of the visit duly arrived. The **Gaelic Ferry** arrived at No. 4 Berth in good time. This was the first obstacle overcome. The next hurdle was the weather. It was a grey and windy day, definitely not the best of conditions for a visit of this nature, but you can't win them all.

One immediate casualty was the helicopter, as we heard from Buckingham Palace about 9.45 a.m. that the Duke was coming by car because of the weather.

The usual last-minute check-up on minor details, a final briefing from the General Manager on the route to be taken on the tour round the ship, vehicles for loading as a

*The **Doric Ferry** at Tilbury terminal, with the P&O Orient liner **Arcadia** in the background. (P&O Library collection)*

*Austin Minis being loaded on the **Doric Ferry** at Tilbury. (P&O Library collection)*

16

*The **Gaelic Ferry** entered service with the Company in 1964, between Tilbury and the ports of Antwerp and Rotterdam. (Nick Robins)*

demonstration were selected. The last-minute instructions given, crates of empty milk bottles and bread trays landed by the ship were hastily removed by the local chandler, and all was ready.

The **Gaelic Ferry** was looking her best, if a trifle damp from the heavy rain. At 10.57 a.m. I joined the party to be presented to the Duke at the foot of the gangway. The rain had kindly stopped but it could start again at any time. At the top of the gangway waited Captain Cowie and his senior Officers.

The Duke was due to arrive at 11 a.m. but, as the clock passed this time and crept slowly forward, it became obvious that even a Royal car can get caught in the traffic, just like any other car.

At 11.30 a pre-arranged telephone call from the Police at the Dock Gate gave the news that the Royal car had entered the Dock. This gave us a "four minute warning", ample time to get our party into a nice straight line in our appointed place.

11.34 a.m. and the Royal car - NGN1 - arrived, escorted by a PLA Police car. Out stepped Prince Philip and apologised to Sir Leslie Ford, General Manager of the Port of London Authority, for being late. Sir Leslie introduced our General Manager, Mr. Michael Bustard, who in turn introduced the Chairman, Mr. F. Bolton. Mr. Bolton presented in turn to the Duke, Mr. Ashley, Mr. Hislop, Mr. Irwin, Mr. Holden and the writer. The Duke shook hands with each, and then asked, "Where are all you gentlemen from?" On being told that they were from Head Office, the Duke said, with some humour, "You are all on a day out today, then!".

Then they went up the gangway with Mr. Bolton to be introduced to Captain Cowie, Mr Lowe, Chief Engineer, Mr. Young, Chief Officer, and Mr. Hastings, Purser.

The introductions over, Prince Philip, who was accompanied by Rear Admiral Bonham Carter and a Police Officer, was escorted by Captain Cowie, Mr. Bolton and Mr. Bustard to the Bridge, Officer Accommodation, Passenger Cabins, Lounge and Dining Saloon. Then through the Crew's Quarters and down to the Vehicle Deck, and lastly the

Engine Room. At each point in the ship, the Shore Superintendent and the Ship's Head of Department acted as advisers and informants to the Duke, who asked many questions and displayed considerable interest in the various aspects of cargo handling and ship's equipment.

From the Engine Room the Duke proceeded up through the ship to the Captain's Cabin, and from there to the top of the gangway, where he bade farewell to the ship's Officers.

Then down the gangway, the Duke moved into No. 4 Shed. Following a brief look round the cargo in the shed, coupled with approving remarks about the amount of Whitbread's beer being shipped by our service, Prince Philip left the shed. He shook hands with Mr. Bolton, Mr. Bustard and myself and was rapidly taken over by Sir Leslie Ford, who was anxious to get our Royal Visitor on to the P.L.A. dock extension scheme. The time was 12.12 p.m. and we had had His Royal Highness in our midst for 38 minutes.

So ended a memorable occasion for those present, and a great honour for the Company and the **Gaelic Ferry**."

The impressive offices of A.S.N. at 25 Whitehall, London SW1. (Author's collection)

On 12th July 1965, the **Gaelic Ferry** opened the new route between the Suffolk port of Felixstowe and Rotterdam. The port of Felixstowe was developed by the Company, in the light of constant labour troubles at Tilbury and also in order that the voyage time to Rotterdam could be halved to six hours at sea.

During 1966, the news came that the Company was to order its sixth vessel to meet the ever increasing demand on their links between U.K., Europe and Northern Ireland.

In August 1966, in order to meet the very critical demand for additional tonnage and prior to the delivery of the new vessel, the Company acquired at an auction at Kiel in Germany another ex-Admiralty vessel. Following the purchase of the ship, renamed **Celtic Ferry**, she was sent to Palmers' Hebburn-on-Tyne yard for alterations including new passenger accommodation and a new upper deck. Her conversion was completed by February 1967 and she undertook trials on 14th February, prior to taking up service on the Felixstowe routes. After only a short period with the company in service, she was laid up during 1974 at Barrow and was sold later the same year.

Probably the best-looking of all the A.S.N. vessels, the **Europic Ferry**, was launched on Tuesday 3rd October 1967. She was not only the largest and fastest vessel ever built for the Company, but was the last A.S.N. ship to be ordered. A detailed feature later in this publication looks at the **Europic Ferry's** career and technical data. Following her launch on the 3rd October at Swan Hunter (Shipbuilders) Limited, Wallsend, the **Europic Ferry** was delivered to her owners on the 29th December 1967, some four months late. She entered service between Felixstowe and the new Rotterdam terminal of Europort at 00.40 on 18th January 1968.

With the arrival of the **Europic Ferry** at Felixstowe, the **Gaelic Ferry** maintained the Antwerp service. The older **Cerdic Ferry** then covered the Tilbury service to Belgium until the 13th September 1968, when A.S.N. withdrew their operations from the Thames port in favour of Felixstowe. The 'Cerdic's' sister **Doric Ferry** was then transferred to

The new terminal building of the Company at Preston was opened during the 'Sixties. (John Jolly personal collection)

the Preston - Belfast service in November 1968.

With a bigger fleet by the 'Sixties and more services to maintain, A.S.N. had to look to other companies for charter vessels during the overhaul periods of the ships each year. It is interesting to note that A.S.N. chose to charter the smart looking and well appointed vessels of Thoresen Car Ferries from Southampton to maintain operations. Two of the vessels were later to come under A.S.N. management at Felixstowe when the Company was taken over by European Ferries.

The charter period of the Thoresen ships usually took place between January and March each year. In 1965, the **Viking II** was used, the next two years the **Viking I**. The chartered Norwegian vessels were used generally on the Tilbury services; however, in January 1967 the **Viking I** served on the Preston - Belfast link.

The Norwegian vessels were able to accommodate about 40 lorries on their vehicle deck; there was no upper deck area

*The **Celtic Ferry** pictured in the North Sea, on passage from Felixstowe to Rotterdam. (Foto Flite 67/6197)*

suitable for the carriage of unit loads. The chartered tonnage was therefore not ideal. It is interesting to note that, while the drive-through vessels were on charter to A.S.N., only the stern doors were used.

During the same year, under the Transport Act of 1968, the ownership of A.S.N. was transferred once again, this time to be a subsidiary of the newly-formed National Freight Corporation.

Operations of A.S.N. stayed on an even keel for the next couple of years, with no major changes in the fleet or the routes.

In 1969, Lt. Col. Frank Bustard became a Freeman of Larne. Some five years later the founder of the Company died, aged 87 years.

The year before A.S.N. was sold out to private enterprise, the Company began to implement plans for the repair of its Cairnryan Pier, on the South West coast of Scotland, following the Company purchasing it in the 'Sixties for £60,000. The pier was to be repaired for a new passenger and freight service to Larne. The development of Cairnryan was eventually to see the closure of Preston, in the light of labour problems at the port and the difficult navigation of the River Ribble. The development of Cairnryan was to take place with the European Ferries Group in 1973. The development and the history of this short sea service is referred to in a later chapter.

As part of the Conservative Government's policy of transferring back into private enterprise those nationalised companies which were viable, A.S.N. and its subsidiaries, the Transport Ferry Service (Nederland) NV and Frank Bustard and Sons Limited became part of the European Ferries Group on the 18th November 1971. European Ferries, better known as Townsend Thoresen, acquired the goodwill of four routes, seven ferries and three terminals for £5.5 million. The sale of the A.S.N. Group took place in the 25th year of the Company's operations.

The take-over of A.S.N. by the European Ferries Group was not to make a major impact immediately. However, the merger of A.S.N. operations with Townsend Thoresen was to take place at the same time as a new era of travel was dawning. Increased passenger and car traffic was to force a change in the style and service of that of the former Company.

*The **Viking II**, pictured here, and her sisters were to become a familiar sight in the A.S.N. service during the winter overhauls of the fleet. (Author's collection)*

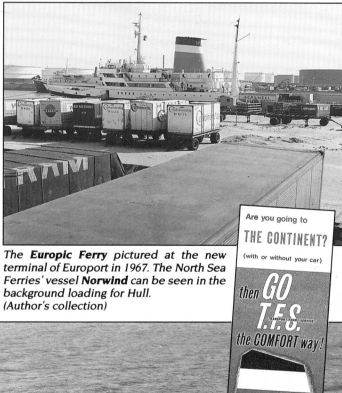

*The **Europic Ferry** pictured at the new terminal of Europort in 1967. The North Sea Ferries' vessel **Norwind** can be seen in the background loading for Hull. (Author's collection)*

Are you going to
THE CONTINENT?
(with or without your car)
then GO
T.F.S.
TRANSPORT FERRY SERVICE
the COMFORT way!

*The **Europic Ferry** on trials in the North Sea. (Author's collection)*

TWO

Taking a Chance

Michael Bustard

The 1920s were not the best years for the United States. They were the years of the Depression, prohibition and the Wall Street Crash. Up till 1923 immigrants had poured in. Then unemployment became unbearable. The doors clanged shut. The result for the North Atlantic passenger trade was disastrous. The bread-and-butter migrant traffic vanished overnight. All that remained was the shrunken First Class passenger trade. It was a bone bitterly fought over, by none more than Cunard and the White Star Line. In 1931 the building of the new Cunard liner No 534, at John Brown's yard on Clydebank, was suspended. In 1934 Cunard and White Star merged - with Cunard taking precedence. One of the White Star Line managers was Frank Bustard, who had joined the company as a traffic apprentice in 1902, a through and through White Star man. Frank Bustard was offered employment with the new merged company but declined in order to start his own shipping line. His idea was not to attempt to break into the overcrowded luxury passenger market, but to create a new no-frills Economy Class with passengers paying extra for meals - but only as consumed. A pay-as-you eat Class. Fare £10 single.

Unhappily the timing of the new venture clashed with the launch of the new Cunard liner **Queen Mary** on which work had been resumed with Government financial assistance. The Government of the day were anxious not to encourage competition with the newly-formed merged company. The

banks were warned off. The ships were never built. But Atlantic Steam had made a start of sorts.

But where and when was the idea of commercial roll-on/roll-off first conceived? It was way back in the dark days of 1943 when the Admiralty carried out beaching trials of the new invasion ships, known as Landing Ships (Tank) on New Brighton Sands. Amongst those present were Lt Col. Frank Bustard, then in charge of the shipment of all military cargoes in the North West ports, and Mr Don Smith of the Liverpool stevedoring firm Smith, Coggins Ltd. As they witnessed the rough wartime birth of what was to prove in later years a worldwide shipping revolution, there was but a single thought between the two visionaries ... why not, when the War is over, use these ships to carry cargo driven on board in lorries? Right from the start Don Smith, an entrepreneur of his time, gave strong support to A.S.N. Tragically, he lost his life at an early age when he died in an air crash at Manchester in 1956.

These ungainly vessels were built in 1943/45 in dozens for the Allied invasions of Italy and France and for the intended invasion of the Far East and Japan. By the Spring of 1946 they were no longer wanted, neither by the Army nor by the Navy. Frank Bustard approached the Admiralty with a request to buy three of these unloved vessels - although at that time it was far from clear where the purchase money was coming from. Although embarrassed by a surplus, the Admiralty were reluctant to sell their LST vessels lest they were required in some future national emergency. Their foresight was remarkable; ten years later all seven LSTs running for A.S.N. were requisitioned by the Government in the Suez crisis of 1956. Negotiations dragged on for months. Finally the Government agreed to let A.S.N. have the use of three vessels, but only on a bareboat charter basis. The rate of hire was agreed at £13-6s-8d per day! All other terms were agreed. But the day was still not won and, before delivery was effected, there was placed in the way one final nailbiting procedure. The Government were anxious to be seen to be even-handed to the fiercely independent shipowners of the day. Accordingly one LST was sent to Tilbury (LST 3511 newly-arrived from Canada under the command of Lt.Cdr. W.N. Johnson R.N.R.) and British shipowners were invited to inspect her and witness a ro-ro demonstration with a view to chartering. A.S.N. held its breath. Unbelievably, the established short-sea and cross-channel shipping lines of that year quickly dismissed the ro-ro idea. Only A.S.N. were bold enough to pursue the new idea.

Much of the credit for this imaginative arrangement of chartering out these vessels can be attributed to James Callaghan M.P., Parliamentary Private Secretary to the Minister of War Transport, himself a "former naval person" who, whilst maintaining at least outwardly a strictly impartial attitude, seemed to be sympathetic to A.S.N. aspirations.

Luck attended the first few weeks. In early August of that first peacetime summer, the Admiralty chose Tilbury as the delivery port for their ugly ducklings-cum-floating garages. This was a most useful start for A.S.N. since it meant the engagement (and expense) of the first Merchant Navy crew could be postponed until the completion of the structural modifications necessary for the conversion from warship to merchant vessel. Naval swords were turned into mercantile marine ploughshares in only three weeks. Crew accommodation was built. The wheelhouse was raised one deck. Port and starboard engine rooms were cross-connected. Lifeboats were fitted. The wardroom became the saloon.

In those days the modern financial catchwords of cash flow and credit control were unknown. If the shipowner's reputation was good then a supply of stores and repairs was provided on credit to an extent which would horrify any modern ship chandler or ship repair firm. Fortunately for

A.S.N., bereft of working capital, Tilbury included a workshop of Harland & Wolff. With this great Northern Ireland company, there existed a strong connection dating back to the pre-war relationship between Belfast and White Star Line. Without their unstinted financial assistance, especially for the conversion of the first three vessels, **Empire Baltic**, **Empire Cedric** and **Empire Celtic**, it is doubtful that A.S.N. would have survived those early anxious days at Tilbury. This frantic initial burst of activity culminated in the first A.S.N. sailing. The **Empire Baltic**, under the command of Captain J. W. Rennie, sailed from Tilbury to Rotterdam with a cargo of vehicles for the Dutch Government on 6th September 1946. It was the first commercial ro-ro sailing in the United Kingdom. Loading was onto a ship's ramp landed on a wartime hard built at No. 26 Berth, and then through the bow doors into the vehicle deck, then known as the Tank Deck. A further internal ramp, precipitously steep, took the vehicles up and onto the Upper Deck.

A truly happy occasion at the retirement party of Captain W.N. Johnson (pictured right) as Chief Marine Superintendent of A.S.N. in October 1972. Captain H.T. Green, the Company's new Chief Marine Superintendent (pictured left) and Michael Bustard share a joke with Captain Johnson of the early days.
(Captain H.T. Green, Retired, collection)

For the next decade A.S.N. was entrusted with the shipment of all vehicles from U.K. to the British Army of the Rhine from Tilbury to Hamburg. Maintained in the early years by **Empire Baltic** (Capt. C.E. Tanner, first Commodore of the Company), by **Empire Cedric** (Capt. W.N. Johnson O.B.E., later Chief Marine Superintendent of the Company) and by **Empire Celtic** (Captain L. Hutchinson). A sailing every two days. The name "Empire" indicated to the whole world that the vessel was in the ownership of the Ministry of War Transport whilst the "ic" name suffix was a kind of official concession to the Company's own nomenclature. This in turn was a nostalgic return to the old former White Star Line ship names ending in "ic". In those days a company's nomenclature was preserved and jealously guarded by British shipping lines. It must be said that the Shaw Savill and Albion Line were, to their credit, also maintaining some of the old White Star Line names. So far, it is not on record what the directors of the Shaw Savill Line thought of this encroachment onto their patch.

Why Tilbury of all places? It must be admitted that there was no shrewd A.S.N. Boardroom decision to opt for this famous passenger port. Already it was the port of embarkation for all Service vehicles and tanks to our forces in Germany. A.S.N. was merely a camp follower. From this start, the new shipping line simply crystallised. Before the arrival of the A.S.N. vessels shipment was painfully effected by lift-on/lift-off means into general cargo vessels, wartime "sam-boats". A ship took days to load and discharge her

cargo of vehicles. The first Hamburg sailings of the new (streamlined) service commenced in September 1946 and continued smoothly into the New Year. Still the A.S.N. luck held. Then the coldest winter in Europe this century tightened its icy grip. The River Elbe froze over from Cuxhaven to Hamburg. As vessels attempted to go upstream they became locked in the ice and as the tide turned from flow to ebb they were gently and helplessly swept downstream in pack ice until the next turn of the tide. The sea water inlets in the Engine Rooms became dangerously choked with ice and main engines were stopped. Days were lost and precious fuel oil wasted. The flow of Army cargoes was slowed down and with it the flow of freight monies.

Ice damage to the bow-door plating was commonplace and had to be repaired in Hamburg before a ship turned round to face the same ice on her return voyage home. The cargo was hardly mobile. Tractors had to tow vehicles ashore before their frozen engines coughed into life. Hamburg was a devastated city. No food. No fuel. The cost of a haircut ashore was two cigarettes. To get the dockers' frozen fingers working a monster stew of old loaves and scraps from the galley was prepared on board on the voyage across to Hamburg. This was ravenously consumed even before discharge commenced; they were desperate days.

Even the route across the North Sea was not easy. Barely twelve months after the cessation of hostilities, it followed what was known as the "swept channel", a route kept clear of German magnetic and acoustic mines laid during the War. Even these precautions did not prevent the mining of the **Empire Baltic** in September 1949. Fortunately she was able to make Emden for temporary repairs and then back to Tilbury.

Despite its gruelling and difficult start the Tilbury-Hamburg service prospered for a further nine years until transferred to Antwerp. Yet, despite the steady stream of traffic, something was missing. Cargoes remained exclusively military with a sprinkling of export traffic. The true laden commercial trailer was absent. Attempts were made to interest the road haulage industry in starting up through services from inland U.K. to cities in Western Europe. All attempts failed. The restrictive blanket of the domestic nationalisation of road transport frustrated all. Attempts to obtain licences to operate Continental vehicles in the U.K. were being prevented by the U.K. licensing restrictions. The only opening in the proposed new "road across the sea" market was the possibility of a ro-ro ferry service between England and Northern Ireland. In September 1948 the Preston-Larne ro-ro service was inaugurated by **Empire Cedric** and **Empire Doric**.

The first few sailings were disappointing. On some nights only one or two vehicles were carried. Traffic was agonisingly slow to build up. But still the ships sailed on... at a loss. It took two years for the traffic to build up to justify a third ship on the service. But why was little known Preston, with all its attendant disadvantages of tidal working, draught and ship length restrictions, chosen to be the English terminal for the new service? Attempts had been made to interest Liverpool but progress here was thwarted by political pressure on the port authority from rival shipping companies already established in the Irish Sea trade. The welcome mat at Preston was shown to A.S.N. Despite its marine handicaps Preston was beloved by the road hauliers of that time. It was already a lynch pin of Northern traffic for the road haulage industry and its vacant dockside coal sidings made perfect vehicle parking areas. A.S.N.'s example was followed by rival shipping companies. Container ship services were mounted by A.S.N. and its rivals to Larne, Belfast, Dublin, Drogheda, Warrenpoint and Greenore. The modest Port of Preston had won its place as the cargo shipping jewel of the Irish Sea for

*The **Empire Gaelic** opened the Preston — Belfast service in 1950. The 'Gaelic' is seen here on passage to Ulster in the early 'Fifties. (Foto Flite 14960)*

some twenty-five years.

In the early 'Fifties whilst the LSTs, which were doing a good job, good enough for the pioneer days, soldiered on, the need to expand and augment the fleet with larger and more economic vessels daily became more critical. The jigsaw pieces of fleet expansion were all there; they only had to be put in place. The ro-ro idea had won acceptance with road hauliers. The ports and routes were established. The ships, albeit less than perfect, were there. Only the money was missing. The Company was desperate for capital. In other words it was undercapitalised. Approaches to the banks were fruitless. "City" resistance to the new ro-ro idea had still not been dispelled. In April 1953 the Company was acquired by the British Transport Commission. (A far-sighted investment move, especially as they had the wit to transfer their newly-acquired A.S.N. shareholding into the name of British Road Services.) At last, the tiny gallant garrison of private shareholders was relieved with honours.

The relationship with the new shareholders proved to be a fruitful one. The Company carried on as before under its original A.S.N. colours, despite the fact that it was a part, albeit a very minor cog, of the nationalised transport undertaking. Its conduct was that of an independent private shipping company. From the day of takeover there was an immediate release of creative energy (and finance) directed to the design and building of new vessels and terminals. No handicaps to expansion were placed in the Company's way. During its seventeen years of nationalised existence, the shareholders financed the building of six new vessels (**Bardic, Ionic, Cerdic, Doric, Gaelic** and **Europic** Ferries) and three new purpose-built terminals at Felixstowe, Cairnryan and Europort.

On the coming to power of the Heath Government in 1969, denationalisation was the order of the day. Many companies fell to the axe in the first hundred days and, in 1971, the Company was acquired by European Ferries. Its structure was maintained intact but with the addition of larger and

faster new vessels, which capitalised and thrived on the potential of the Felixstowe and Cairnryan routes.

Despite, however, the full-every-night sailings across the Irish Sea, there remained nagging thoughts in the A.S.N. mind. Whilst the road hauliers had successfully established themselves and were quite content to remain in Preston, A.S.N. was still left grappling with its nautical difficulties. The draught restrictions, often acute at neaps, in the River Ribble were becoming a problem. The ship length restrictions of the entrance locks were limiting the desired optimum size of new vessels to replace the outgrown LSTs and, most important of all, the length and time of the crossing militated against improved ship utilisation.

As the months and years busily passed by at Preston, a great opportunity through sheer good luck arose in South West Scotland. It was the then unknown port of Cairnryan, built during the War as No. 2 Military Port. This secret port was used for the loading of ammunition ships for our forces overseas. After the War its only visitor was the occasional vessel dumping ammunition in the North Atlantic; it went to sleep. It was then sold to Mr. Pounds, the Portsmouth shipbreaker, who in turn sold it to Queenborough Shipbreakers after disposing of a large number of cranes to the East African Railways.

In the early 'Sixties, A.S.N. began secret negotiations with Mr. Pounds to acquire part of his Loch Ryan empire. These culminated when the A.S.N. Board, albeit with some well-concealed misgivings, showed great foresight in purchasing 10 acres, known as the Lighterage Wharf, out of Mr. Pounds' Scottish estate of 200 acres. Mr Pounds was well satisfied with his sale of a near derelict wharf to a shipping line who were ready to pay £25,000 for waterside land in a remote part of South Western Scotland. Ten years were to pass until the new A.S.N. Cairnryan-Larne service was inaugurated by the **Ionic Ferry** on 10 July 1973. The effect on A.S.N.'s Irish Sea economics was electric. At a stroke the shortest sea crossing between U.K. and Ireland gave A.S.N. a round voyage ship utilisation of a few hours compared to the previous 48 hours out of Preston. Once again the concept of bridging the ocean at its narrowest point proved unbeatable.

In the meantime the main jetty, over three thousand feet long, became the final resting place for many famous aircraft carriers, including H.M.S **Ark Royal**, and other warships. Surprisingly, and despite its name, the firm of Queenborough Shipbreakers was in Italian hands and was owned by a diminutive, bird-like and courteous gentleman by the name of Mr. Gandini of Genoa, who paid occasional visits to the U.K. to oversee his shipbreaking empire at Cairnryan and Queenborough and at the same time to confer with A.S.N. on their respective and potentially valuable quay. It was vital to A.S.N. that a friendly, business-like relationship be maintained with its neighbour.

By 1952 the Northern Ireland service was at last paying its way. Two more LSTs, **Empire Doric** and **Empire Gaelic**, had been acquired from the Admiralty but two obstacles blocking the path to further expansion remained firmly in place. Whilst commercial ro-ro to Northern Ireland had been enthusiastically taken up by the road haulage industry, there was no such explosion to the Continent. All efforts by A.S.N. and their road haulier customers to break into the Continental market were resisted by the quota system of licensing. This arrangement adhered to by all European countries permitted only a trickle of laden British trailers/vehicles onto the Continental roads. The extension of the ro-ro revolution into Europe was in danger of being strangled at birth. Then two happy changes of direction took place. From its inception the service into Germany formed a vital part of the B.A.O.R. line of communication from the U.K. to our forces ranged in front of the Iron Curtain. The lifeline to our forces in Hamburg only 20 miles from the East German border was vulnerable. The military thinking, quite correctly, was that the line of support should come from behind an army, not in front of it. Accordingly, the route was switched into Belgium. The Port of Antwerp served a great traffic catchment area. Voyage time was halved. The cheaper tractor haulage

charges in the Benelux countries acted as some kind of catalyst to the British hauliers. Hamburg had been too far. Belgium was nearer ..... and cheaper. In 1957, A.S.N.'s new streamlined service was the first commercial ro-ro service into Belgium, followed by the mounting from Tilbury of the first ro-ro service into Rotterdam - again the first commercial ro-ro service into Holland.

Traffic mushroomed. There was even a waiting list for shippers. New ships were being built. Profits were being made. But still nagging thoughts, doubts and misgivings could not be silenced. The ocean was not yet bridged between its narrowest points. The search for a shorter route, if not the shortest route, into the Benelux countries was mounted.

The then little-known Port of Felixstowe was "discovered" by A.S.N. in the early 'Sixties.

Nothing was found wanting - except for a ro-ro terminal. This was promptly and willingly provided by the Felixstowe Dock and Railway Company. A.S.N. were to become the golden key that unlocked Felixstowe. The new service into Holland was inaugurated by the **Gaelic Ferry** on 12 July 1965. It never looked back. The service into Belgium was concentrated on the Felixstowe - Zeebrugge route in 1974. At that time few of A.S.N.'s haulage customers had even heard of Felixstowe's existence and many were loath to leave their comfortable Thames-side bed to pioneer into unknown East Anglia, but a good haulier will drive over broken glass to find the right port and the cheapest sea route ..... and they did. To their credit they followed the fleet into Felixstowe.

Michael Bustard
Tonbridge, Kent

*The **Ionic Ferry** in the River Ribble approaching Preston Dock in September 1966. (Nick Robins)*

THREE

Life and Times with A.S.N.

I went to sea aged 16 in 1936 as an apprentice with A. Holt & Co. of Liverpool (The Blue Funnel Line) with whom I remained until early 1948. Having married after the War and wanting to be nearer home, I joined the Irish Lights Service, responsible for the maintenance of lights, buoys etc. round the Irish coast. This was considered a safe and secure career in those days, but the pay was minimal and, having seen the A.S.N. ships running into Larne, I sent in an application. I did this against much advice, being assured that neither the ships nor the Company would survive very long or, if it did and I ever became Master, the hazards of Preston and the River Ribble would have me in an early grave.

I joined the **Empire Cedric** in September 1949 under Captain Johnstone and after a few months transferred to the **Empire Gaelic** under Captain H.T. Green where I remained until promoted Master of the **Empire Doric** in 1954.

The conditions of employment were very good. There was a reasonable wage (£48 a month I think). Generally on the coasting trade in those days one supplied one's own food or paid the cook to do so, but in A.S.N. catering was provided.

Initially one ship left either side on Monday, Tuesday, Thursday and Friday, spending Wednesday night and Saturday to Monday in port. As trade increased sailings became every week-day so that each ship did three round trips per week.

What helped to consolidate the service in the early days was the contract to transport over 2,000 aluminium pre-fabricated houses to Northern Ireland. Each was loaded onto its own trailer and provided a two-way traffic, as the empty trailers had to be returned.

The initial years up to 1956 were a time of great job satisfaction. One was aware of contributing to the success of a new venture and almost every week another customer would arrive. A great deal of the traffic was by companies using their own transport, and their vehicles were generally immaculate, in showroom condition. The drivers were company employees of long standing usually in a smart uniform and travelling weekly year after year.

The voyage in the LSTs could in itself be quite an adventure. Normally the overall passage time was about 14½ hours. The sea passage was about 12 hours at 10½ knots and 2½ hours were spent negotiating the River and locks, arriving at or departing from Preston.

In bad weather it could take much longer. The LSTs had a very quick rolling motion. To minimize this and protect the cargo it was the practice to keep heading into the sea until

Captain W. Close

one could turn the ship as quickly as possible bringing the sea astern. This might add many hours to the passage. One frequently had to run for shelter and we must have anchored in most of the various bays in the Irish Sea.

It was essential on rounding the Chickens to have a good idea what conditions would be like on arrival at Preston Bar. In a North Westerly gale the entrance was considered unapproachable, and one doubted if an LST would turn round under these conditions - certainly not without a great deal of cargo damage. If in any doubt one anchored under the Isle of Man and awaited a moderation.

A Winter voyage could last for days rather than hours. I think a week was the record for a round voyage. However, this was generally accepted philosophically by all concerned. There was considerable satisfaction in having, as it were, weathered the tempest and attained a safe anchorage, there to await it blowing itself out.

Navigation of the Ribble commenced at the Gut buoy about 16½ miles from the dock entrance. The channel was enclosed by retaining walls for much of its length. It was marked by buoys at the entrance and lighted perches for the rest of its length. In the early days many of these were lit by paraffin lamps like those on a Victorian railway platform. After a strong blow many would be extinguished to be re-lit

Empire Cedric on passage to Preston. (Author's collection)

A British Road Services lorry pictured on the deck of **Empire Cedric** in the 'Sixties. (Author's collection)

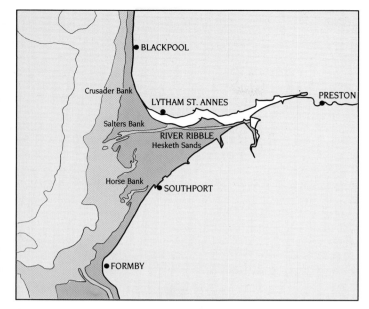

*The **Empire Nordic** in the lock at Preston Harbour, outward bound for Northern Ireland in July 1966. (Paul Clegg)*

in a leisurely fashion by the "lampies" whose sole job it was to maintain them.

One arrived at the Nelson buoy about two hours to high water and the River passage and locking in varied from 1½ hours to three hours depending on the state of the tide, other traffic etc., but normally lasted about two hours.

Negotiating the stretch from Wallend buoy to Lytham in a West to North Westerly gale was an unforgettable experience.

A very big breaking sea developed over the Bar and one had to be very alert and sure of one's judgement to clear the sandbanks to the North and avoid being carried over the Wall to the South by leeway and tide which, once the wall and banks were covered, ran strongly in an East-South Easterly direction. Keeping as close to Salters buoy as possible one made about a 30° alteration to port to avoid the South bank which was liable to encroach into the channel, and shortly after a similar turn to starboard. Often, after bad weather, one of more of the buoys would be missing and the seaward perch demolished, so that one was compelled to judge the position by keeping the bearings of perches open to clear the wall.

It was an exercise which could not have been attempted without confidence in the ship, one's local knowledge and the ability of the quartermasters to steer accurately a given course.

It was a great relief, but very satisfying, when one gained shelter approaching Lytham and could take in the stabilisers.

After Lytham the River became canal-like and the main concern was outward traffic, sand pumps or often a combination of both.

The upper reaches were surrounded by extensive marshes on both sides. On a calm summer's morning these would be covered by low-lying mist above which showed the tops of solitary trees giving an unreal impression of a world of primeval swamps at the dawn of time. At that time there was a great variety of bird life, and year after year it was the place I heard larks for the first time, in early Spring.

The Ribble required constant dredging but, even with this, silting was a recurring problem. After a long dry spell the soundings would be 6' or more less than the datum. In anti-cyclonic conditions the tide would be cut up to another 2'0" so that on a neap tide of 19'6" there would be a maximum of 11'6" of water. By restricting cargo it was possible to sail the ships at about 11'6", and on a few occasions they were neaped in for a tide or more.

The only remedy for clearing the Ribble was a really long period of heavy rain in the Pennines when the fresh would rise to 15' and clear the channel overnight.

The upper reaches of the Ribble were much inclined to be hampered by fog in certain conditions, particularly in the early days when Preston was very much a Lancashire mill town. If visibility were known to be very bad we would not sail or attempt to enter, but often conditions would worsen on passage. However, there were surprisingly few mishaps, again mainly due to very competent quartermasters and the ability one developed with the radar.

In August 1956 all the ships were withdrawn literally at a few hours' notice for the Suez operation.

Although this episode certainly had its element of variety and interest, one remembers it as a period of anxiety, confusion and frustration.

I remember the period of about 1958-1970 as really the heyday of the Preston service, with ultimately three purpose-built ships giving six sailings weekly each way with 'Bardic' and 'Ionic' to Larne and three sailings to Belfast with 'Doric'.

There was great pride taken in the maintenance and appearance of these ships. They were a study in polished brass, varnished teakwork, and holystoned decks. The engine rooms were cream paint, brasswork and burnished steel.

During the Summer months the passenger accommodation was invariably booked out and customers certainly got their money's worth. Nothing like it had ever been experienced in cross-channel travel before and certainly not since.

The ships did of course provide a much better year-round service and were not nearly as liable to weather delays as the LSTs.

The first and, I think, the only Atlantic Steam Navigation Company vessel to cross the Atlantic was the **Cerdic Ferry** in

*The **Bardic Ferry** under tow in the River Ribble. (Author's collection)*

Main picture: The **Europic Ferry** was delivered on the 29th December 1967. She was the largest and fastest ferry ever built for the Company. The **Europic Ferry** is seen here in the New Waterway off the Hook of Holland on her morning sailing to Felixstowe. (J. Zevenbergen collection)

Top left: The **Gaelic Ferry** entered service in January 1964, initially from Tilbury. On 12th July 1965, the 'Gaelic' opened the new Felixstowe — Rotterdam service. (Foto Flite CN 2368)

Top right: The twin funnelled **Celtic Ferry** at Felixstowe in August 1969. (Andrew Jones)

Left: A peaceful evening scene at Felixstowe in October 1971, with **Europic Ferry** and the **Cerdic Ferry**. (Andrew Jones)

Top left: A view of the Antwerp terminal with the **Cerdic Ferry** loading for Tilbury.
(Author's collection)

Top right: The **Doric Ferry** entered service at the end of April 1962 on the Antwerp and Rotterdam links from Tilbury. The 'Doric' is pictured here at Tilbury in the morning sun, following her arrival from Antwerp.
(P&O Library collection)

Centre: The **Ionic Ferry** pictured at Preston during her first season in service on the Northern Ireland link in 1958.
(P&O Library collection)

Left: Two of the coasters of the A.S.N. fleet, **Linda** and **Elisa** laid up at Preston in the Sixties. The **Linda** usually operated the Dublin service, while the **Elisa** maintained the Larne cargo link.
(M. Hibbert)

*An evening view at Preston with **Ionic Ferry** loading for her sailing to Larne. (Author's collection)*

*Evan Cook's transport lorry on the quayside at the Port of Preston with **Bardic Ferry**. (Author's collection)*

1970 on a charter to run between Nova Scotia and Newfoundland for Canadian National Railways. It gave me great pleasure as Master to send Colonel Bustard a telegram on passing Cape Race informing him that, after so many years, one of his vessels had actually crossed the Atlantic.

During 1969 a long dock strike occurred in Preston, when the ships ran quite successfully from Barrow-in-Furness. A great deal of Preston's success had been due to its good labour relations, and after this the confidence in the service never seemed quite the same again. The closure of Preston was probably inevitable, given modern conditions, but I think this was the beginning of the end for the Port.

Thus the venture to open Cairnryan - Larne was very much welcomed. All concerned worked very hard to make it a success and there was at that time great goodwill towards the new venture by the travelling public. It was said by some of our competitors that neither the berth nor the service would survive the first winter, but they were proved wrong.

During 1971 A.S.N. operations were taken over by the European Ferries Group; the new management quickly endorsed the earlier decision to move from Preston to Cairnryan.

On 24th March 1973 the Preston - Larne service was closed, ending a very happy association for me with the Lancashire port. The **Ionic Ferry** was then taken up to Cairnryan for berthing trials, after which she returned to Belfast to undergo modifications. Some cabins were removed and passenger seating substituted to increase her capacity to 219 passengers. The new service opened on 10th July 1973 and was to become well-patronised over the years.

No shore staff were employed at either side in the early days of the service, therefore unaccompanied vehicles were not carried. As trade increased it became necessary to employ shore staff at both terminals.

During the period between 1973 and 1984, I was Master at various times of all the vessels which served between Larne and Cairnryan, mostly on the **Free Enterprise IV** and finally on the **Europic Ferry**. Schedules on this route, each ship completing three round trips in 24 hours, made what was virtually a shift system inevitable and three Masters were employed for each ferry.

Previous to this, like most other Masters, I had been appointed to a ship and remained there, in my case on the **Ionic Ferry** for 13 years. This was by no means unusual, as the ship almost came to be regarded as the personal property of the Master, an attitude which I think was encouraged by the management. Certainly very few from Colonel Bustard downwards would have gone anywhere on board without having the Master accompanying them, and permission was always requested first before visiting the bridge.

From 1976 I was employed on the **Free Enterprise IV**. This vessel offered very different passenger accommodation to that of my earlier commands with the Company. Most of

*An aerial view of the Port of Larne in the 'Sixties. The **Ionic Ferry** is seen here between two of the coasters of the A.S.N. fleet, pending her evening sailing to Preston. The British Railways steamer **Caledonian Princess**, second from the right, has just arrived from Stranraer. (Larne P.R. Archives)*

*The **Ionic Ferry** moves slowly away from the quay at Preston, with the aid of a tug, under the command of Captain W. Close. (Paul Clegg)*

*The **Cerdic Ferry** at Port aux Basques, Newfoundland in July 1970. (Captain W. Close, Retired)*

her modern passenger accommodation was open plan, with extensive seating areas and a large bar. The vessel offered no little cosy corners for passengers to sit quietly and talk, like the old A.S.N. vessels. Nevertheless the **Free Enterprise IV** was to prove a very successful vessel on the link with the travelling public. Had we had one of her other sisters from

Dover too, I am sure we would have been a formidable challenge to the other short-sea service from Larne.

During my last eighteen months prior to my retirement, I served on the magnificent **Europic Ferry** which I thoroughly enjoyed. It gave me one last feeling for the very excellent ships of A.S.N.

The everyday ferry operations of the 'Nineties of Larne are still with me, as I am lucky enough to live on the sea front. As I enjoy my retirement, I can watch the **Europic Ferry** and her operating partner the **Ionic Ferry** glide in and out of the port on their daily routine.

I am proud to have served with the Atlantic Steam Navigation Company and everything that it has given me. Those early days will never be forgotten.

Captain W. Close
Larne

***Free Enterprise IV**, inward from Scotland, passes the **Europic Ferry** off Larne Harbour. (Ken Kane)*

The **Gaelic Ferry** was to remain in service until December 1986. The former A.S.N. ship is seen here leaving Portsmouth for Le Havre in Townsend Thoresen livery and following her lengthening in 1972. (Andrew Jones)

The **Cerdic Ferry** laid-up in Ramsden Dock, Barrow in April 1981, prior to being sold by European Ferries. (Bernard McCall)

The **Viking Viscount** and her twin sister **Viking Voyager** pass each other in the North Sea, while maintaining the Felixstowe — Zeebrugge service in October 1976. (Foto Flite 11846)

The **Free Enterprise IV** was transferred from Dover to the Larne — Cairnryan route in May 1976. The 'FE IV' is seen here leaving Larne for Scotland in June 1977. (Larne P.R. Archives)

F O U R

The Doric Ferry Angling Club

Some few months after I joined Transport Ferry Service in March 1969, I was transferred from the Felixstowe service to the Preston - Northern Ireland route, Preston being quite close to my home in Blackpool. This started what was to become a very happy relationship for the next few years, until the Port of Preston was finally closed down in 1978 by a cost-cutting Town Council (although the ferries had already left Preston by then), thus ending a marriage in commerce, forged by the late and great founder of A.S.N., Colonel Frank Bustard and his family.

Going to work in ferries after some twenty-three years sailing to all parts of the world with larger passenger companies, one wondered quite what to expect, certainly some diminishing of service and possibly standards? But no, emphatically no! Reduced numbers, yes - but reduced standards, no. The ships running from Preston to Northern Ireland, as with those engaged in the Felixstowe and Continental services, were ferries ahead of their time. The small roll-on/roll-off ships were well-maintained, of neat appearance and had excellent standards of accommodation and catering. No expense was spared in keeping this small but highly efficient fleet ahead of any competitors and, as with the standard of the service, the Company ensured that they employed the best staff qualified to run them. Higher Grade Certificates were a must or, where certificates were not required, a good background and impeccable references from a well-established company!

All in all, it gave the necessary ingredients for a happy working relationship and, at the time, a great deal of job satisfaction, something one hears little of in an ever expanding industrial world; as the adage still goes "Small is

Beautiful!" It was truly a great pleasure to work for such a Company and the happy relationship spread to all corners of the system, between Superintendents, Port Officals, River and Dock Pilots, Customs and Immigration Officers, Cargo Clerks and all the people involved in running the day-to-day affairs connected with such an endeavour.

Not least of these happy relationships were the friendships that developed between regular passengers and, more notably, the regular weekly commercial drivers who plied between England and Northern Ireland. Such regulars as the I.C.I. drivers who drove their tankers from Teeside to Newry and other parts of the province. Shaw's Carpets from Yorkshire and Riding's, the Preston-based firm, were well known to us. Dennis, the man who drove the "Battery Wagon" from the Midlands, he of the rich tenor voice who regaled the drivers' Clubroom with song on the evening crossings. The regular Holt-Jackson Library Stockists' driver became known as "The Book-Man"!. So, many of them became good friends as well as customers, and we always looked forward to meeting up with them on crossings. In fact, I think it's true to say that they took as much pride in travelling on the ships, as we did in running them!

Which brings me to the title of this tale - "The Doric Ferry Angling Club." The vessel was at that time under the command of the late Captain Rupert Hockings. "The Hock", as he was more widely known to his crew, was pretty much every man's idea of a perfectionist, a very definite person who did not suffer fools gladly, to put it mildly. He was a good seaman, he knew his ship well and handled her with great skill, a fact with which I'm sure many who served with him will agree. Due to the nature of the service, night crossings were at varying hours because of the tidal conditions prevailing at Preston; working hours were very unsettled and one made full use of rest periods. It was during such periods that the **Doric Ferry's** "Unofficial" Angling Club came into being. It started with one or two dedicated fishermen such as Retired Commodore Chief Engineer Freddie Price, the late Fourth Engineer George Walmsley, and "The Hock" himself. Whilst anchored off the Nelson Buoy in the Ribble Estuary, awaiting high water to take us up to Preston Dock, there were usually two or three hours to kill after the trip across from Belfast

The Doric Ferry on trials in April 1962. (Author's collection)

Lough, and these intrepid few were out on the after deck, whatever the weather, lines cast from the stern, patiently waiting for the cod to bite, but usually bringing in a few plaice or dabs, with the occasional whiting or large skate coming up over the ship's rail! This was, at first, a source of great amusement to the rest of the crew, passengers and drivers alike! But on good days when the mackerel were running and coming over the rail sometimes five or six on a trace, the "knockers" soon forgot their snide remarks and then joined in the fun! After some time had passed it became more and more difficult to find a position on the rail to fish from, and there would be a mighty rush to get into a good position once the anchor chains had stopped rattling. Anyone who had finished work for the time being would be out there, jostling for the best position.

It wasn't long before our regular commercial drivers were purchasing rods and tackle and bringing them along to join in the fun, and another step from there to storing the rods on board with the crew members'. Who knows what would have happened if an erring Transport Manager had re-routed them down South, to London or Wales, or elsewhere! One could imagine the chagrin, the black looks and excuses being made by the drivers to stay on the Irish Sea crossing!

The main source of obtaining bait was from Belfast Lough, where king-sized ragworm could be found in the heavy clay that made up the foreshore near to our berth in Herdman Channel, and again a roster was drawn up of those who were available to go digging. Boiler suits and wellies being the rig of the day, and armed with garden spades, the diggers (including drivers who were waiting for the next sailing) would set forth merrily down the foreshore to search for ragworm, carrying cans and jars to hold them. I well remember an occasion when an irate Night Engineer was heard loudly swearing and complaining bitterly because someone had stored packets of ragworm next to his supper sandwiches in the duty mess fridge! It was only a further step in gaining angling experience, whilst the **Doric Ferry** lay alongside in Belfast on a sunny afternoon, to be invited to take part in a boat drill, which involved taking the motor launch down the Lough to the Fairway Buoy. Suitably attired in life-jackets and then dropping the sea-anchor and really getting among the mackerel!

Many a laugh was heard over the telling and re-telling of the story of Fred Price (one of our more expert anglers) who, on one occasion came back from leave with some up-to-date information that the best method of attracting cod was to use a deflated red balloon! We could hardly wait for the next lifeboat drill in Belfast to try out this theory. Armed with our

*A stern view of the **Doric Ferry**. The **Doric Ferry** made her maiden voyage on the Preston — Larne service in February 1962, prior to taking up the Tilbury — Antwerp/Rotterdam link with her sister the **Cerdic Ferry**. (Nick Robins)*

fishing gear and bait, including red balloons, we set off down the Lough to the Fairway Buoy. On arrival there we all held our breath as Fred fed pieces of balloon onto the hook at the end of his line and then cast his line! No one can ever tell exactly what happened at that precise moment, but Fred, wearing his shorts, disappeared over the gunwhale of the boat and, though many say they definitely heard a splash, Fred almost immediately re-appeared back over the gunwhale, completely dry and also completely unnerved! We swear he actually went out of sight for about five seconds, it was quite incredible and, as John Williams the Radio Officer remarked later, he always thought Fred walked on water!

However, we found out on that trip that red balloon is one of the finest lures for catching mackerel ever devised, as well as silver paper, chocolate wrappers or any other old trash!

On innumerable occasions we returned to Preston and landed many sacks of fish on the quayside for our office staff and dockers to help themselves, after we had selected the "cream of the catch!"

Happy days, enjoyed by all. Some of the relationships that were forged between drivers, passengers and crew still exist to this day. We were advertised as "The Friendly Service to Northern Ireland" but it's easy to make friends working under the conditions which existed then. However, the demands of progress in commerce soon caught up - expansion through take-overs, bigger ships and busy schedules soon ended the idyllic way of life enjoyed by us all. Though, as I said previously, some of those friendships cemented on crossings of the Irish Sea still continue. This was confirmed to me when, some four or five years ago, I was contacted by "Fred the Books", one of our commercial drivers mentioned earlier, asking me to stand as Best Man at his marriage to an Irish lass, met on his trips through the Port of Larne! I was more than happy to oblige!

Hugh P. Ghee
Senior Purser (Retired)

FIVE

A Port is Born

THE EARLY DAYS OF FELIXSTOWE

I joined Atlantic Steam Navigation at Larne on 28th May 1948 just a few weeks after the commencement of the first ro-ro service between the mainland and Northern Ireland. It is true that there had been a lot of previous ro-ro activity in the port of Larne, but mainly passenger and car traffic on the Stranraer to Larne route and also during the War, when many of the train ferries had been converted for the carriage of military equipment. I had first worked at Larne Harbour at the end of 1944 and can well remember the continual comings and goings of **Shepperton Ferry, Twickenham Ferry, Royal Daffodil, Empress Queen, Hampton Ferry** and many others. When I arrived in Felixstowe in early 1965 as Port Manager it was to find a terminal very much in the course of construction, a derelict office which had been the old RAF Met. Office and a note to "get on with interviewing staff" for the various jobs available. This proved to be a very interesting task as we had made a conscious decision not to employ anyone with previous shipping experience. We had applications from 180 people, all of a very high standard, from whom I had to pick just ten. I am pleased to say that five of the original men are still with the Company, two of them in managerial positions.

Transport Ferry Service commenced operations out of the Port of Felixstowe on 12th July 1965. The vessel employed was **Gaelic Ferry**, capable of carrying 65 commercial vehicles and with accommodation for 28 drivers and passengers. She was scheduled to make three round trips per week, arriving at Felixstowe Mondays, Wednesdays and Fridays at 21.00, sailing again at 23.30. At this time we were still running up river to the Port of Rotterdam, but our eventual objective was to allow the ship to make a round trip every day. This was achieved with the completion of the new terminal at Europort, cutting down the passage time from nine to seven hours. In this way the Company was able to double ship utilisation when compared to the old Tilbury operation. The fact that Continental time was one hour in advance of ours was a distinct advantage to us in keeping to our schedule!

Even in the early days, space was at a premium. Over 2,600 cars had been delivered to us for shipment two weeks before the first ship had arrived! The terminal at Felixstowe consisted of five areas of hardstanding, a berth with a 32-ton crane and a floating pontoon with two bridgespans, each capable of carrying vehicles up to seventy feet long, ten feet wide and weighing up to 120 tons.

We also had a 20-ton mobile crane, with outriggers for trans-shipment work, on the quayside. Tugmasters were not available to us at that time; our shunting units were a collection of second-hand AEC, Leyland and Commer equipment which were to prove very efficient, despite being a constant source of trouble to the garage responsible for our maintenance. It should be said that as time went on we did rectify this situation, gradually building up one of the largest and best fleets of Tugmasters in the country, together with over 200 slave trailers for containers.

The original terminal lent itself to expansion and it has now grown to approximately 35 acres with parking space for around 700 × 40' units. The pontoon is now double-decked for three-deck working and in addition the Company has added a second two-deck ramp and berth to accommodate the Zeebrugge service.

In 1965 Felixstowe was very well equipped for transit sheds. The departure of the RAF left three very large

Mr. Sid Livingstone

hangars, one of which was allocated to us for the inspection of import and export goods. Much work had to be done to ensure that everything came up to H.M. Customs and Excise requirements, not least the construction of an enormous cage in which high value goods had to be off-loaded for examination.

Felixstowe in the late 'Sixties. Cars on the quayside awaiting export. (P&O European Ferries' Library)

*An aerial view of the Port of Felixstowe in the early 'Seventies, with the **Gaelic Ferry** loading for Europort. (Paul Clegg collection)*

Complications arose because it was our intention to use existing annexes to the hangar for temporary office accommodation to house the staff of our customers. Every wall had to be lined with a solid wire mesh, with the boltheads and nuts welded so they could not be removed. All to ensure that no unauthorised persons had access, and to allow Customs control at all times.

At the time of moving to Felixstowe from Tilbury, A.S.N. made a decision to provide as much land for development as possible. Space would be needed for International and National Haulage. One plot of sixteen acres and another of seventeen acres were leased from The Felixstowe Dock and Railway Co. and Trinity College, Cambridge. It must be said that this decision had much to do with the success of A.S.N. at Felixstowe; being able to offer this land for depots and office accommodation attracted many top companies to the port.

In those early days everyone around the dock was convinced that we would do well, but there were some in the area who felt that general cargo was still the thing and that, in any case, Tilbury would be the major ro-ro port for many years. How wrong they were. We carried 17,000 units in our first full year to Rotterdam and in 1989 that figure had risen to 160,000 commercial units. Tilbury survived just 18 months after we left.

Co-operation in the early days was outstanding. Everyone on the port worked very hard to produce the sort of service that would attract customers. Mr. Ian Trelawny and his assistant Ted Hall were particularly helpful to us, spending many hours helping to sort out all the problems that go with the introduction of a new service.

Those pioneering days of the 'Sixties of the Port of Felixstowe were eventually to create one of Britain's major harbours over the next 25 years, handling containers, ro-ro traffic worldwide and cars with their passengers to Europe. Those early days of 1965 are still remembered by many who worked and lived around Felixstowe. For me personally those were some of the happiest years of my life, with many memorable occasions in which I was to make many friends.

S. Livingstone,
Suffolk, November 1990

*Felixstowe in the 'Eighties. The **Cerdic Ferry** gets underway for Europort. (Bruce Monaghan)*

SIX

Gaelic Ferry
A TOUCH OF CLASS

The **Gaelic Ferry** on passage from Felixstowe to Europort in July 1965. (Foto Flite F/33)

For years, the Atlantic Steam Navigation Company fleet has been known for its rather special passenger accommodation but, due to my isolation in darkest Kent, I had long given up the idea of being able to enjoy a leisurely sail in one of its diminishing number of ferries.

When, rather unexpectedly, Townsend Thoresen switched the 22-year-old **Gaelic Ferry** to Dover in July 1985, I was determined that, even though a crossing to Zeebrugge seemed impossible to arrange, I should at least attempt a viewing of this rather special ship.

My opportunity came in mid-November when, after crossing from Calais to Dover with my friend Miles Cowsill, we were duly shown down to one of the port's original berths where the **Gaelic Ferry** had just docked .

The single linkspan was up on her upper deck and we crossed the vast open vehicle space, where a few minutes before lorries and "drops" had been sandwiched together before entering her accommodation on the promenade deck.

A crew change was in progress (the ship had three crews working on a rota of 24 hours on, 48 hours off with 32 in each crew) but, on hearing why two strangers had boarded their vessel, an unbelievably warm welcome awaited us. We were soon to find that enthusiasm for the ship was not just the province of armchair sailors like ourselves.

All those I spoke to and had the privilege of meeting had volunteered for duty aboard the ship and some had obviously endured considerable ribbing from their colleagues in the modern Townsend Thoresen fleet. None of them however had regretted knowing the **Gaelic Ferry** and had immediately fallen in love with her undoubted charm, quality, sturdiness of build and happy atmosphere. They agreed that they would never forget this most excellent vessel.

After a quick look round the empty passenger accommodation - the "Gaelic's" 12 passenger spaces were invariably taken by lorry drivers who had been known to wait as long as eight hours in Zeebrugge in order to sail in her - we met Captain Chris Double who invited us onto the bridge.

What a sight for sore eyes this turned out to be! No large electrical consoles full of flashing lights, numerous buttons and gadgetry. No space-age wizardry or carpeted decks but instead a timeless wheelhouse with a teak deck on which stood the essentials and a splendid, large, brass wheel. There was no automatic steering of course; in the **Gaelic Ferry** it was hand steering all the way and, at 13 knots, that meant between 6½-7 hours. In bad weather, the speed could be reduced to as little as eight knots when she would be too slow for her fin stabilisers to act and then life on board could be very interesting.

With all the freight away, Captain Double invited us to stay on board while he took the ship away from No. 2 berth to dock at the nearby lay-by berth in the Camber. With the "Gaelic" being the longest ferry at Dover and with reinforced concrete walls surrounding her, Captain Double joked that

The **Gaelic Ferry** was launched at Messrs. Swan Hunter & Wigham Richardson Ltd. on 3rd October 1963 by Mrs. F.B. Bolton. (Author's collection)

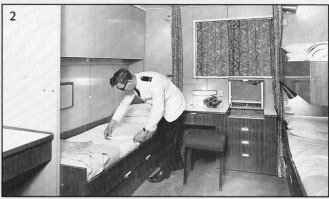

Gaelic Ferry

1. The Dining Saloon. (John Hendy collection)
2. A view of a 4-berth cabin. (Author's collection)
3. The Clubroom for lorry drivers. (Author's collection)
4. The handsome looking **Gaelic Ferry** at sea in the 'Sixties. (Author's collection)
5. Engine room control area in the **Gaelic Ferry**. (Miles Cowsill)
6. Looking aft on the main vehicle deck. (John Hendy)

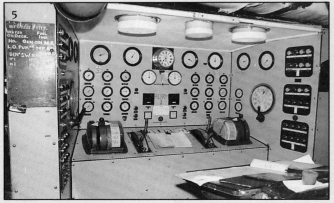

he was pleased that there was not one breath of wind and that the sea was of mill pond character but it never ceases to amaze me how *easy* the Channel masters make it all seem.

Close at hand was First Officer Vic Ridges who was, perhaps, the "Gaelic's" greatest fan. A keen collector of ship postcards, Vic had contacted Foto Flite for copies of their excellent photograph of the vessel and had found a ready market for these on board.

After the brief move across the Camber had been accomplished, Purser Darryl Chaffey took us down into the engine room where we were shown around by Third Engineer Campbell Ferguson. One was immediately impressed by the lack of noise and by the spaciousness of the area. As the **Gaelic Ferry's** twin Sulzer diesels were slow-running, they were easy to maintain although spare parts were a problem by then and the original-sized cylinder rings no longer fitted her.

Unlike the modern ferries, the commands from the "Gaelic's" bridge were "telegraphed" into the engine room in the traditional way and her engineers found this aspect of her operation as enjoyable as their colleagues in the deck department.

It is of interest to record that, while the ship was loading and unloading, the screw shafts were always kept turning in order to prevent fracture in case the movement of heavy freight lorries above caused the ship to sag.

The **Gaelic Ferry** was undoubtedly needed at Dover after the **Free Enterprise VI** and then the "VII" went away to Bremerhaven for "jumboising". She was particularly useful for carrying "drops" (trailers without motors and therefore requiring to be shunted by small tractor vehicles) and thus she allowed the three "European" class freighters to take normal loads and therefore keep to timetable.

Everyone felt that she must have paid for herself many times over but, with an already extended 20-year safety certificate, the feeling on board was that the Company would not consider it worthwhile spending a lot of money on her in order to bring her back into Class. A shame, yes, but economic factors outweigh all others in today's shipping scene.

The **Gaelic Ferry** was built in the West Shipyard at Swan Hunter and Wigham Richardson and was launched into the Tyne on 3rd October 1963. Her sponsor was Mrs. F.B. Bolton, wife of the Chairman of the Atlantic Steam Navigation Company.

As originally built, the ship was 2,760 gross tons, measured 365ft. × 56ft. × 13.5ft. and twin 2-stroke single acting 10-cylinder Sulzer engines drove her at 16 knots. The installation had a total continuous output of 5,200 shp at 300 rpm although revs were down to 270 in the ship's later life.

She entered service on the Tilbury to Antwerp and Rotterdam routes in January 1964 under the command of

*The **Gaelic Ferry** in drydock at Belfast undergoing her annual overhaul. (Larne P.R. Archives)*

Captain J.W. Cowie, and on 24th March the ship received a visit at No. 4 berth at Tilbury from H.R.H. Prince Philip, Duke of Edinburgh — an honour indeed both for the new ship and for the Company.

From 12th July of the following year, she was switched to the Suffolk port of Felixstowe from where a new service to Rotterdam was opened.

Press releases at the time tell us that the **Gaelic Ferry** was able to carry individual bulk loads of up to 180 tons in new Boden semi-trailers on a thrice-weekly service leaving Felixstowe on Mondays, Wednesdays and Fridays and returning on Tuesdays, Thursdays and Saturdays. British Road Services stated that there would be a reduction in crossing times of 16½ to 9½ hours comparing Felixstowe with Tilbury together with an anticipated speed-up in Customs clearance. On her inaugural voyage on the new route, the "Gaelic" loaded a large consignment of BMC cars which were carried in her special lower deck, beneath the main vehicle deck. In January 1966, the new ferry also opened the new Felixstowe — Antwerp link.

The **Gaelic Ferry** was originally fitted with passenger accommodation for just 28 which was finished to a high order with much wooden panelling throughout. There were many examples of the craftsmen's work which helped give the ship an individual atmosphere and above all a degree of "style" which I certainly felt immediately I entered her accommodation. As with all the A.S.N. ships, the "Gaelic" was advertised as First Class and this was certainly no exaggeration for on the leisurely services on which their ships plied passengers they were to meet standards which were second only to those found on the better class of Atlantic liner. And this, of course, was what the Company founder,

*The **Gaelic Ferry** at Felixstowe on 19th April 1979. (Ambrose Greenway)*

A view of the "Gaelic" arriving at Larne in 1984. (Ken Kane)

The Gaelic Ferry in the Camber at Dover in 1985. (John Hendy)

Frank Bustard, would have wished.

With the final A.S.N. ship **Europic Ferry** on station in January 1968, the labour-troubled Tilbury services were gradually run down until their closure in September that year.

The **Europic Ferry** maintained the Rotterdam link while the "Gaelic" kept the Antwerp service running, but the increase in traffic on the Dutch route saw the earlier ship switched there as from January 1971 when the Belgian passage was down-graded to freight-only.

Later in the year, the nationalised Company was sold to the European Ferries Group for £5.5mn. Eight ro-ro vessels were involved in the deal and the new owners soon announced plans to develop Felixstowe along the lines of Dover and Southampton.

In February 1972, the **Gaelic Ferry** was sent back to Swan Hunter's at North Shields to receive an extension to her passenger accommodation raising numbers from 28 to 44. This meant an addition to her superstructure in the area of the funnel so that both her mainmast and her lifeboats were now "stepped" to stand on the new cabins.

An even more significant change occurred to the ship during March 1973 when she was again sent back to her builders to be lengthened by 76ft. This work gave her increased capacity for 200 commercial vehicles a week and reflected the tremendous boom in roll-on/roll-off traffic. Trials were carried out on 17th May and the, now rather awkward looking, ship left for Felixstowe on the following day.

Although such ship-surgery is now fairly common, it was a major operation in those days and the "Gaelic" must have been one of the first ro-ro ships to have her life extended by such work.

The multi-purpose vessel **Viking II** commenced the new Felixstowe — Zeebrugge route on 23rd October 1974, the new **Viking Valiant** joined her on 21st May, while the following November the **Ionic Ferry** joined her former A.S.N. consorts on the Europort link.

Further steps in the expansion of Felixstowe occurred when the **European Gateway** entered service in June 1975,

and on 9th March 1978 the **Viking III** commenced operation on the Rotterdam service offering for the first time a seven-hour, tourist-type passage to Holland. It was not a success and represents one of the few European Ferries ventures to end in failure.

The previous Autumn had seen the former Atlantic Steam ships finally and inevitably lose their smart livery of black

Looking aft from the bridge on the Gaelic Ferry. (Miles Cowsill)

The "Gaelic" pictured at Southampton with the second linkspan being lowered on board. (Author's collection)

hull with white line, and blue funnel topped by black and white bands. Instead, the uniform Thoresen orange hull with green funnel was applied.

In early 1980, European Ferries introduced the chartered Stena vessel **Nordic Ferry** to work alongside the "Europic" and the "Gaelic" and it seems that both the earlier ships had their accommodation extended from 44 to 60 berths.

Over the Christmas of 1980, the "Gaelic" however was laid-up at Tilbury and she appears to have been there for some months and even offered for sale.

The ship was later reactivated and in mid-November 1981 was replacing the **European Gateway** on the Cairnryan — Larne link. There now began a somewhat nomadic life which characterised her later career.

The Summer of 1982 saw the **Gaelic Ferry** laid-up at Barrow before the Falklands conflict brought her southwards to Southampton to deputise for the "Europic" which had been called-up for "active service". Then when Felixstowe's **Nordic Ferry** and **Baltic Ferry** were also called up, the "Gaelic" was switched back to her old route on the 2nd May while the **European Gateway** arrived to assist on the following day.

European Ferries hastily chartered the **Wesertal** and **Dima** followed by the larger **Syria** and **Hellas** (from Stena) which allowed the "Gaelic" to take the service from Southampton to Le Havre as had originally been planned. The pattern of Cairnryan for the Winter and Southampton for the Summer had been set although, with the decline of

operations at the Hampshire port, Portsmouth was substituted as from the 22nd May 1984.

At the start of 1985 the ship was back at Cairnryan but with the takeover of P&O Normandy Ferries and a sudden surplus of tonnage, a large question mark was placed over her future employment. Lay-up was again at Barrow where she was expected to be offered for sale. The shortage of tonnage at Dover, due to the stretching programme, happily saw her rescued for one final stint and, when she arrived at Dover in early July 1985, she took up a daily 21.30 Zeebrugge sailing arriving back at 16.30 every afternoon. Sundays were often free when the ship would lay-up in the Camber.

The ship was due to finish on 21st December and Bulgarian owners inspected her with a view to purchase. However, a strike at Dover saw the faithful "Gaelic" finish on 13th December, after which she was sent to Chatham to lay-up.

One more task awaited her. During the Spring of 1986, the ship's deck fittings were stripped and she was towed as a dumb barge to Southampton's Princess Alexandra Dock where two redundant linkspans were lowered on board. The "Gaelic" was then towed back to Zeebrugge, the intention being that the "cargo" should be used to construct the port's first double-decker linkspan. She arrived at the Belgian port on 25th April where she was moored in the inner harbour to await her destiny.

However, it was another Townsend Thoresen ship which was to determine the future of the **Gaelic Ferry**. In the company of the **Flushing Range**, she was towed away for scrapping in Taiwan on 5th October 1987, sailing under the flag of St. Vincent and Grenadines as the **Gaelic**. Both vessels broke free from their tug during hurricane force winds in the Bay of Biscay and in the Indian Ocean before they were eventually relocated and again taken in charge. The port of Kaohsiung was their final destination and this was reached on the morning of 22nd March 1988.

For the **Gaelic Ferry**, it was a sad end to an exceptional career.

John Hendy
Staplehurst

*A sad end to a fine lady. The former **Gaelic Ferry** is towed down the English Channel in the Autumn mist on passage to the breakers. (Foto Flite 1-64349)*

SEVEN

The Coastal Fleet Operations of A.S.N.

The Port of Preston played a crucial role not only in the successful growth of A.S.N. during the 'Forties and 'Fifties, but also in the early development of unit load and containerised cargo. A.S.N. was one of four operators to sail from Preston, the others being Anglo Continental Container Services (ACCS), Northern Ireland Trailer Services (NITS) and Greenore Ferry Services (GFS).

In fact the Dutch coasters **Noach** and **Prior** were the first container - carrying coasters to visit Preston and they arrived for ACCS in 1954 and 1955 respectively.

Container and other unit loads were, of course, handled regularly by the seven former tank landing ships which had been working between Preston and Larne or Belfast since 1948. In 1956, the Ministry of Transport requisitioned the "Empire" ships and A.S.N. was compelled to charter conventional coasters in their stead. The vessels' cargo-handling derricks were unshipped and stored on the dock, thus giving easier access to the holds and leaving more space for deck cargo.

The first coasters to be chartered by A.S.N. were J and A Gardner's **Saint Kilda** (708 gross tons) which arrived at Preston on 22nd August 1956 light from Glasgow and sailed for Larne four days later, and John Monks' **Cliffville** which also sailed for Larne on 26th August. The **Saint Kilda** charter ended on 21st September but **Cliffville** continued until 19th January 1957. A third vessel, the Irish **A. R. Rawall**, had a three-week charter until mid-September.

Between mid-September and January 1957, three larger West German vessels were chartered, the **Kapt. Jan Reinecke** (1489 gross tons), **Fidentia** and **Heinrich Lorenz**. They were joined by **Mary Robert Müller** on 24th October.

From mid-January 1957, the "Empire" vessels began to return from Suez duty and the only container vessels working out of Preston were those chartered by ACCS or NITS.

The **Loch Etive** leaving Preston in A.S.N. colours. *(Paul Clegg collection)*

The **River Fisher** in the Ribble in July 1966. *(Paul Clegg)*

Arriving on 16th January for ACCS was a brand new Dutch vessel, the **Biscaya**. Within three weeks, she was renamed **Elisa**. She is important in our story for she inaugurated A.S.N.'s first container service on 1st January 1960. On the following day, the Dutch vessel **Goodwill** arrived from Larne and these two ships continued to connect Preston and Larne on alternate days throughout 1960.

With trade building up steadily during the year, the **Prior** had to be chartered from ACCS occasionally. By mid-August, it was clear that extra capacity was required on a regular basis so James Fisher's **Stream Fisher** was chartered, her first voyage being on 24th August.

In mid-1961, a brand new vessel joined the service, the Dutch **Goodwill Trader** (500 gross tons) which sailed to Larne on 22nd June. Like the **Prior** and **Goodwill,** she was owned by A. C. Hoff whose vessels were to play an important role in A.S.N. container services. In December 1961, **Stream Fisher** began a new service to Drogheda, departing on 18th December. For most of 1962, the **Goodwill** and **Goodwill Trader** sailed on alternate days to Larne, while the **Stream Fisher** and **Noach** sailed on alternate days to Drogheda. The **Goodwill** was replaced in December by the new **Goodwill Merchant**.

By the Spring of 1963, further developments were afoot. The Irish vessel **Inniscarra** was taking containers to Dublin for B+I, and included some voyages to this port for A.S.N. The official A.S.N run to Dublin was inaugurated in March by **Stream Fisher** and she was soon joined by **Elisa**. The **Goodwill Merchant** and **Goodwill Trader** operated the Larne service, while the **Prior** looked after the Drogheda run. During July 1963, the **Prior** was renamed **Trinitas**.

Later in 1963, Fisher's **Bay Fisher** (1289 gross tons) came onto the Dublin service, releasing the **Elisa** to return to Larne traffic. Traffic on the Dublin service was building up too, and by mid-1964 the **Race Fisher** was chartered in to operate the link. In September 1964, A.S.N. began to serve a fourth Irish port when the Dutch **Friso** began sailing from Preston to Waterford.

By the end of 1964, trade on all routes was flourishing. Larne needed four vessels, the **Goodwill Merchant, Goodwill Trader, Elisa** and **Race Fisher**. The Dublin route was served by the **Trinitas** and **Stream Fisher**. The **Friendship** came onto the Drogheda service later in the year. Extra sailings for Dublin were handled by the **Loch Etive**. The Waterford service was entrusted to the Irish vessel the **Loch Linnhe;** although she really was not suitable for conveying unit loads. Trade had now outstripped the ability to provide suitable ships.

*The **Coria** at the T.F.S. Berth, Preston in November 1968. (Paul Clegg)*

Not surprisingly, with trade expanding rapidly, 1965 saw several newer vessels chartered in by the Company. Fishers provided **Leven Fisher** (1540 gross tons), **Eden Fisher, River Fisher** and **Firth Fisher** at various times, and there was to be considerable interchange of ships between routes. Larne generally needed five ships, and as a rule it was the Dutch ships which worked on this route.

Dublin required three ships, and these tended to be Fisher vessels. The **Derwent Fisher** (1096 gross tons) arrived from her builders in Groningen in March and immediately joined the Dublin service. The sailings to Drogheda were in the hands of the **Clipper**, owned by A. C. Hoff like the "Goodwill" ships, and the **Noach**, and a further Dutch vessel, the **Fastnet**, was running the Waterford service.

Between mid-May and early July 1966, all services to Dublin ceased. This was due to a dispute involving Fisher vessels; other ships were not affected. During July 1966 the Waterford service ceased, largely so that trade could be concentrated on the three most successful routes.

New, purpose-built ships at last began to arrive on the routes. In November 1966, Hoff's **Goodwill Traveller** arrived from her builders in Groningen. With a capacity of 54 TEUs, she had the biggest capacity of all the ships chartered thus far.

In early 1967, Shamrock Shipping Ltd. of Larne took delivery of the sister ships **Curran** and **Moyle**. They immediately joined the Irish Sea services from Preston with the **Moyle** being used on A.S.N.'s Larne service and the **Curran** being used on Coast Lines' routes after just one voyage for A.S.N. This was her first commercial sailing - to Larne in February. She joined the A.S.N.-chartered fleet in September. When more modern ships were not available, it still proved necessary to charter older ships. Thus the **Loch Etive** was back on the Larne run at the end of 1967 and for the Drogheda service the **Noach** had **Cambrian Coast** as her running partner.

When the West German **Barbel Bolten** arrived in Preston direct from her builders at Travemünde on the morning tide of 19th January 1968, the A.S.N. container service began to enter a new league. She was over 20 metres longer than **Goodwill Traveller** and, more significantly, was four metres wider. As a consequence she could stow containers in four rows instead of three, and she boasted an 88 TEU capacity. She departed for Larne on the morning of 20th January, and records show that she carried 728 tons 5 cwt of cargo on her maiden commercial voyage. The veteran **Loch Linnhe** had been taking about 185 tons only three years previously. Such was the true extent of the container revolution, once purpose-built ships were developed.

On 22nd January, another new ship arrived. She was the **Orwell Fisher** and came direct from Rotterdam. Slightly longer and beamier than **Barbel Bolten**, she had a capacity of 85 TEUs and began service on the Dublin run although she transferred to Larne in May.

Another significant development in January was the launch of a service to Belfast, inaugurated by the **Coria**. Traffic soon built up and two vessels were needed to handle the cargo on offer by the Summer. In June, the **Solway Fisher**, the sister ship of the **Orwell Fisher**, arrived at Preston from Rotterdam on the 3rd, and commenced work on the Larne route. The **Barbel Bolten** too was joined by a sister ship in mid-June; this was **Marietta Bolten** and her maiden commercial voyage to Larne was on 21st June.

With the arrival of these two ships, it was possible to release the **Cambrian Coast** from charter. She had been working on the Drogheda service and was replaced by the **Goodwill Trader**. All chartered ships were now relatively modern, having been built in the 1960s and just four owners were involved. A.C. Hoff provided the **Goodwill, Goodwill Merchant, Goodwill Trader** and **Goodwill Traveller**. Also from Holland, Dammers and Van der Heide supplied the **Coria, Elisa** and **Linda**. West Germany was represented by Auguste Bolten's the **Barbel Bolten** and **Marietta Bolten**, and the U.K.'s two representatives were James Fisher's **Orwell Fisher** and **Solway Fisher**.

Not surprisingly, the four newest vessels - the two "Boltens" and the two "Fishers" - were allocated to the Company's premier Larne route where they remained until 1972.

The only items of note in early 1969 were the charter of **Pool Fisher** for two round voyages to Dublin in May, and the return of the **Marietta Bolten** to her builders in July, presumably for guarantee work.

In August 1969, the Irish Sea services were dealt a crippling blow when Preston dockers went on strike on 7th August and did not return to work until 20th October. This tarnished the image of the Port of Preston. Many foreign trades left the port and Irish Sea traffic failed to reach earlier levels

In January 1970, the **Solway Fisher** arrived light from Pasajes on the 9th and sailed light to Liverpool on the 19th, suggesting lack of work or charter problems, and by March the Larne service was being maintained by the two "Bolten" ships with only occasional help from other vessels. There were nine ships working the four A.S.N. routes, the **Goodwill** having been released in August 1968 and **Elisa** in December.

1971 saw an unusually settled period of operations. The Larne service was operated by the **Barbel Bolten, Orwell Fisher** and **Solway Fisher**, Dublin was served by the **Coria** and **Goodwill Traveller,** and Belfast by the **Linda** and **Goodwill Merchant. The Goodwill Trader** coped single-handed with the Drogheda work, while the **Marietta Bolten** was used to support the Belfast and Larne services as necessary. During the early part of 1972 two very significant events were to occur. Firstly, at the end of July, Preston dockers took further industrial action in support of jailed London dockers. This strike lasted well into August and there were no A.S.N. sailings at this time. Secondly, traffic on the Larne route slumped.

By December, the **Goodwill Traveller** could cope with all that was on offer, although the Belfast route was proving somewhat busier.

By 1973, the A.S.N. container service was in obvious decline. Some of the vessels found themselves sublet to other users; the **Goodwill Merchant,** for instance, spent the whole of May working to Drogheda for Coast Lines. On the morning tide of 19th June, the **Barbel Bolten** arrived from Larne and then sailed to Hamburg on the next tide, her charter having been ended.

The **Goodwill Merchant** loading at Preston. (John Jolly personal collection)

Her sister ship arrived at Preston from Belfast on 30th June and remained at Preston until 18th August when she departed light for Kiel.

Early 1974 began with just four ships in service - the **Linda** and **Coria** were working to Dublin while the **Orwell Fisher** and **Goodwill Traveller** were serving the Belfast link. It was announced in the "Lancashire Evening Post" on 31st January 1974 that the ferry service to Larne would cease at the end of April. In fact there had been no A.S.N. container sailings there for several months. To make matters worse, the **Goodwill Traveller** suffered a fire which damaged her galley and messroom while at Preston on 10th March. In July, she found herself trading to Londonderry for both Coast Lines and A.S.N.

The next year witnessed a brief revival, although it was also to witness some farewells. The **Moyle** reopened the Larne route briefly in January, and the **Goodwill Traveller** continued to serve Londonderry. She made her final A.S.N. sailing from Preston on 30th January. The **Solway Fisher** and **Orwell Fisher** worked regularly to Belfast, and the **Linda** and **Coria** maintained the Dublin service. However, the **Coria** made her last sailing on 26th June and was replaced by the **Moyle.** Meanwhile the **Curran** joined the Dublin run in mid-November.

The next farewells came at the end of December 1975. The **Solway Fisher** made her final sailing to Belfast on 28th December and the **Orwell Fisher** closed the service when she departed on the next day. Both ships continued to serve Belfast but from Heysham. They kept their A.S.N. colours although now working for Containerway.

By January 1976, the only A.S.N. service from Preston was that to Dublin maintained by the **Curran** and **Moyle.** Very surprisingly the **Linda** returned to join them for an eleven-day spell in November.

On 8th February 1978, the **Curran** made her final A.S.N. voyage to Dublin, and the **Moyle** departed to Dublin for the last time on 13th March. However, this final A.S.N. route was not to close just yet for the **Owenglas** had begun service on the route two days earlier. In May, she began to use Greenore as the Irish terminal. She maintained this new route single-handed apart from an eleven-day period in December when she went to Liverpool for dry-docking. Her place was taken by the **Guernsey Fisher.**

With the **Owenglas** back in service, her return proved very short-lived. She departed for Greenore on 31st January 1978 and that was the final A.S.N. voyage from Preston. Thus ended a chapter of vital importance not only to the development of Irish Sea trade but also to shipping history in general. The growth of unit load and container traffic owes much to A.S.N.'s pioneering developments at Preston.

Bernard McCall

Bernard McCall

EIGHT

The Townsend Thoresen Association

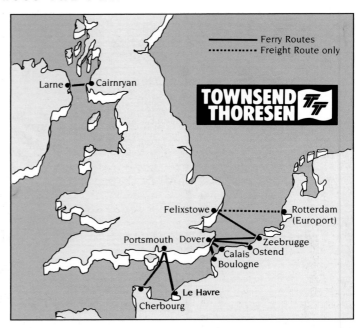

As part of the Conservative Government's policies in the early 'Seventies, A.S.N.'s operations were sold to the European Ferries Group on 18th November 1971, for £5.5 million. European Ferries, better known to the travelling public as Townsend Thoresen, acquired the operations of A.S.N. to Ireland and the Continent and their seven ships.

Prior to their acquisition of A.S.N., Townsend Thoresen was operating four Continental routes. The trading company of Townsend Thoresen had been formed in 1968, when Townsend Car Ferries and Thoresen Car Ferries had joined forces to create Europe's largest independent ferry operator. Both individual companies, prior to their merger had gone into direct competition on the English Channel, against the established services of British Railways and S.N.C.F.

The Townsend side of operations began in 1928, when Mr Stuart M. Townsend attempted to bring an end to the monopoly held by the Southern Railway Company on the English Channel. The new Company initially opened their service between Dover - Calais using a small coaster. Some two years later, the Company acquired and converted a former minesweeper to expand their operations. The new ship was to be renamed **Forde** and was to remain in service on the Dover - Calais link until 1949.

The early operations of Townsend Car Ferries were to be only crane-loaded, as the port authorities on both sides of the Channel were not in favour of the Company building a linkspan for cars to be driven straight on board. However, during the French General Strike in 1936, the cranes at Calais were strikebound and as the **Forde** already had a stern gate, she was able to take cars on board directly off the quay. These events were eventually to lay the foundations of the ferry operations we have today.

Continued growth during the 'Fifties prompted the Townsend family to go public. The share issue was launched on the very day that the Egyptian Government announced

Free Enterprise III arriving at Cairnryan from Larne on 30th July 1974. (Paul Clegg)

The distinctive livery of A.S.N. was to disappear during 1976, in favour of the Townsend Thoresen orange hull with a blue funnel. The **Doric Ferry** *is seen here arriving at Larne in the new livery. (Author's collection)*

that they were going to nationalise the Suez Canal. Trading on the Stock Market slumped as a result of this announcement, and only a few shares were sold. Meanwhile a group of Coventry businessmen were searching the Stock Market for a small company with large assets which they could transfer to their own organisation. Mr George Nott and his partners took a controlling interest in the Kentish shipping company and later voted out the Townsend family.

It was the intention of the new owners to strip Townsend Car Ferries of their assets and close the ferry service completely. The new management fortunately saw sense and the Dover - Calais service continued, producing some handsome returns with the **Halladale**, which had entered service during 1949.

The new management of Townsend looked further afield to increase the profits of their shipping operations during the late 'Fifties. During 1959, they chartered the former tank landing craft **Empire Shearwater** to open a rival service to that of A.S.N. between Tilbury and Antwerp. The new link was only for lorries and offered a cut-rate alternative to the established Tilbury route. In the event the new service was to last only six months.

During the early 'Sixties, Townsend Car Ferries began to make major inroads on the Dover Straits, against their rivals British Railways and S.N.C.F., when their first purpose-built ferry **Free Enterprise** entered service in 1962. In March 1966 the **Free Enterprise II** opened the new Dover - Zeebrugge route for the Company. Following the opening of the Zeebrugge link, the Company was to expand at a rapid rate between 1966 and 1974, during which time six more new ferries were built for the Dover operations.

Meanwhile, during May 1964, the first of Otto Thoresen's Norwegian "Viking" ships entered service on the Southampton - Cherbourg route. Later the same year, on 20th July, the **Viking I** opened the Le Havre service, even though British Railways claimed at the time that the route was uneconomic. The Thoresen vessels with their orange-painted hulls and their well-appointed passenger accommodation were to set a trend and standard for British ferry companies over the next decade.

In 1968 both companies joined forces as Townsend Thoresen, out of which the European Ferries Group was born.

Following the take-over of A.S.N. operations by the European Ferries Group, the distinctive fleet of 'The Transport Ferry Service' was to remain intact for a further couple of years. The high standards of service and operations created by A.S.N. management were sadly to decline during the 'Seventies, following their take-over, in the light of economics and changing passenger needs.

The days of passengers leaving their cars at the gangway and being met a by a white-coated attendant, who drove your car on board and left your vehicle on the quay for your disembarkation at your leisure, could no longer be maintained. The very high standard of catering facilities and the excellent quality of service on board were also adapted to meet the mass travel concept.

Following the take-over, the new management quickly took the decision to move from Preston to Cairnryan, in the light of poor industrial relations and sailings being restricted by the tides at the Lancashire port.

A new terminal and linkspan had to be developed to handle the new service at the small Scottish village of Cairnryan on the edge of Loch Ryan. The original **Ionic Ferry** was chosen to open the new service as from 1973.

The **Ionic Ferry** was sent for a refit, following the Preston - Larne service closing on 24th March 1973. During her refit two extra lifeboats were fitted aft, which enabled her passenger certificate to be increased from 55 to 219 passengers. The crane on the upper deck was removed, which allowed the upper deck area to be used for passengers' cars and lorries.

On Monday 10th July 1973, the **Ionic Ferry** opened the new service under the command of Captain W. Close. Initially the **Ionic Ferry** sailed twice a day from Larne at 09.00 and 16.00 with sailings from Scotland at 12.30 and 19.30; this schedule allowed the **Ionic Ferry** to lie overnight in Ulster.

Following the closure of the Preston - Larne service, the Preston - Belfast link was increased to a daily service each way with the **Bardic Ferry** and **Doric Ferry**. The Belfast route

*The well-appointed **Viking II** opened the Felixstowe - Zeebrugge route on 10th October 1974. (Foto Flite H17)*

was to be abandoned a year later on Saturday 29th July 1974 in favour of the now well-established Larne - Cairnryan service.

During early 1974, work on a second linkspan and a new marshalling yard was started at Cairnryan. In the meantime, on the Irish side, European Ferries bought the entire share capital of Larne Harbour Company Limited in October 1973, to enable them to consolidate their position at the port.

Following the take-over of A.S.N., European Ferries continued to use the former trading name of the Company, "The Transport Ferry Service", for the next three years to advertise the former routes. During 1974 the trade name of Townsend Thoresen was introduced to market the services, in conjunction with the TFS household name.

In Spring 1974 the news came from Dover that **Free Enterprise III** (4,656 gross tons) would be transferred to the Irish service as from 1st July. The new ship for the link would provide drive-on/drive-off facilities and would join the

Ionic Ferry for the Summer.

The **Free Enterprise III** did indeed enter service on 1st July, with a scheduled crossing time of 1 hour 45 minutes; in the event she was to need just under two hours to complete her crossings. With a capacity for 250 cars and 1,200 passengers in one class, the **Free Enterprise III** was to make a sudden and dramatic change to the link. The Townsend vessel made a great impression on the route and, at the end of her Summer spell on the link on 21st October, she returned to Dover. Her place was taken for the Winter period by the **Bardic Ferry**, which now had received the same modifications as her sister.

At the Suffolk port of Felixstowe operations were not to change dramatically following the take-over of A.S.N. The first major investment in the Felixstowe operations came during 1974, when it was announced that the Antwerp service would be closed in favour of the Port of Zeebrugge which had been used by Townsend Car Ferries since 1966.

*The **Viking Voyager** and the **Viking Viscount** were to maintain the Zeebrugge route until 1986, when both Felixstowe-based "Super Vikings" were transferred to the Portsmouth - Cherbourg service. The **Viking Viscount** is seen here outward-bound from Felixstowe during her first season in service. (Author's collection)*

*An impressive view of the **Europic Ferry** swinging off Felixstowe. The "Europic" was joined on the Dutch service in June 1975 by the **European Gateway**. (Ambrose Greenway)*

Two new ships were ordered in Denmark for the Zeebrugge link at the same time as new tonnage was ordered for Southampton. The four new vessels were to become known as the "Super Viking" class and were to be modelled on the "Vikings" built by Otto Thoresen in the 'Sixties and the "Free Enterprise" ships at Dover. The cost of the four new Viking ships was some £20 million. The "Super Vikings" with their twin funnels would be able to carry 1,200 passengers and 275 cars on two decks when completed. The first of the "Super Viking" ships, the **Viking Venturer**, entered service during January 1975 between Southampton and Le Havre.

The new Felixstowe - Zeebrugge service was opened initially by **Viking II** on 10th October 1974. The second of four new "Super Viking" vessels, the **Viking Valiant**, was placed on the link as from 21st May 1975, with the **Viking II**. The **Viking Valiant**, originally earmarked for Southampton - Cherbourg/Le Havre services, remained on the new route until the arrival of the third new vessel, **Viking Voyager** in January 1976. On the arrival of the last "Super Viking", the **Viking Viscount**, the **Viking II** was then withdrawn from the route and later sold.

The two new "Super Vikings" quickly established themselves on the Felixstowe - Zeebrugge route, maintaining the link with three sailings each daily around the year. During the overhaul periods most years the 'Viscount' and 'Voyager' were covered by the **Free Enterprise IV** from Larne.

Meanwhile it was also announced in 1974 that the third of the "European" class vessels currently being built in Germany would be put on the Felixstowe - Europort link when completed, with the **Europic Ferry** as from the next year. On 9th June 1975, the **European Gateway** made her maiden voyage between Suffolk and Holland. The "Gateway" was to remain on the Dutch service until 1981.

The Summer schedules for the Larne service in 1975 initially did not make provision for a passenger car ferry as in the previous year but, with a lull in the strife in Northern Ireland the **Free Enterprise I** was transferred to the link from Dover for the Summer period only. The first of the "Free Enterprise" class vessels was not to prove a success on the route and did not return again to the Irish Sea.

The next year **Free Enterprise IV** was switched from Dover to the route as from May 1976. She was to become a great success and firm favourite on the link for the next ten years.

During the next couple of years the **Doric Ferry** and **Cerdic Ferry** were to be the operating partners with the **Free Enterprise IV** on the Ulster service.

During September 1977, for a six-month period, the **Viking Viscount** was switched to the Dover - Zeebrugge route in order to cover the overhaul periods at the Kentish port. Her place was taken by the chartered **Stena Nordica** for the winter period on the Felixstowe - Zeebrugge route.

On 9th March 1978 a new passenger service between Felixstowe - Rotterdam (Europort) was opened by the former Thoresen ship **Viking III**. The new service operated from the Dutch port at 23.59, with a return sailing from Felixstowe at 14.30 daily.

The **Viking Victory**, from Portsmouth, took over the route during October to allow the **Viking III** to try out another new service between the Scottish port of Leith and Kristiansand in Norway for the rest of the year.

The Europort passenger route sadly was not to be a success and closed; also the Leith-Kristiansand link was not to be repeated in 1979.

During March 1980, the **European Gateway** was transferred from Felixstowe to cover the dry-docking period of **Free Enterprise IV** and the **Doric Ferry** until June.

A new double-deck link span was completed at Cairnryan during 1980, thereby allowing double-deck loading at both the Scottish port and Larne.

In September 1980 the **European Gateway** was sent to Amsterdam Dry-Dock Company for lengthening by 15.7

*The **European Gateway** captured in the morning sun at Felixstowe, prior to her sailing to Europort. (Author's collection)*

Above: The **Viking III** at Felixstowe pending her afternoon sailing to Europort. The **Viking III** opened the passenger service to Holland on 9th March 1978. (Author's collection)

The **Free Enterprise IV** pictured at the Continental Quay, Larne in November 1980 following her morning arrival from Cairnryan. (Rodney MacKenna)

Below: The **Free Enterprise IV** in dry-dock at Belfast undergoing her refit. (Larne P.R. Archives)

metres to increase her freight capacity and add additional passenger areas. Following her lengthening, her passenger certificate was increased to 326.

Meanwhile, during 1981, the **Cerdic Ferry** and **Doric Ferry** were withdrawn from service and offered for sale. The **Europic Ferry** was transferred to the Southampton - Le Havre freight run on the arrival of the larger Stena-built vessels **Stena Transporter** and **Merzario Hispania** (6,455 gross tons), later to be renamed **Baltic Ferry** and **Nordic Ferry**.

The **European Gateway** returned to the Ulster link again in 1981 following her lengthening for nearly a year with the **Free Enterprise IV**. The **Free Enterprise IV** and the **European Gateway** were to enjoy a very good reputation both with freight operators and passengers. During late 1981 the Company were considering withdrawing the **Free Enterprise IV** from the link and operating it solely with the **European Gateway**. Fortunately these proposals were not implemented, as it would have severely damaged public confidence in the Company's route.

On the night of Sunday 19th December, the **European Gateway** was lost off Felixstowe in a collision with the **Speedlink Vanguard**. Her place was quickly taken by the **Europic Ferry** from Southampton. With the loss of the **European Gateway**, the **Gaelic Ferry** was transferred to the Northern Ireland link until March 1983, when she was replaced by the **Europic Ferry**.

The Falklands War broke out during Spring 1982, and the **Nordic Ferry** and **Baltic Ferry** were requisitioned by the MOD for service in the South Atlantic. With the departure of the "Nordic" and "Baltic", their original sisters **Hellas** and

The **Cerdic Ferry** at Felixstowe during her last season in service. The **Cerdic Ferry** and the **Doric Ferry** were sold in 1981 for further service in the Mediterranean. (Ambrose Greenway)

48

*The Norwegian built car ferry **Viking III** commenced the new passenger service between Felixstowe and Europort on the 9th March 1978. The new link closed the following year due to poor response. (Foto Flite CN 20323)*

*The **Nordic Ferry** pictured prior to her conversion to a passenger ferry in 1986. (Foto Flite 1/12514)*

*The **Viking Voyager** on passage to Zeebrugge. (Foto Flite 81500)*

The **European Gateway** arriving at Cairnryan during her first season on the Ulster link. (Author's collection)

Syria were chartered to cover the Europort service.

During October 1985, European Ferries decided upon a major re-development of their fleet at Portsmouth, Felixstowe, Larne and Dover.

It was decided that, as from 1986, the **Viking Viscount** and **Viking Voyager** would be transferred to Portsmouth, to operate with the newly-jumboised "Super Vikings", **Viking Venturer** and **Viking Valiant**.

The "Super Vikings" would be replaced by the **Baltic Ferry** and **Nordic Ferry** on the Zeebrugge route. Both would undergo conversion to passenger and freight ships the following Winter before re-entering service. Meanwhile the Europort service would be covered by the long-term charter of the **Syria** and **Hellas** from Stena Line.

At Cairnryan, **Free Enterprise IV** would be transferred back to Dover to operate with the **Free Enterprise V** on the Boulogne route; her place would be taken by the **Dragon** from Portsmouth.

An impressive view of the **Nordic Ferry** at Felixstowe.
(Bruce Monaghan)

The **Nordic Ferry** and **Baltic Ferry** underwent their £5 million refits during the Winter in 1986 to provide luxury accommodation for 650 passengers for their new role. Both ships did not have the speed of the "Super Vikings" and therefore the service on the route was reduced to two round sailings a day, instead of the original three sailings. The introduction of the **Baltic Ferry** and **Nordic Ferry**, however, increased the freight capacity on the route by 30 to 160 units per sailing.

On the departure of the "Baltic" and "Nordic" for conversion the **Hellas** (renamed **Doric Ferry**) and **Syria** (renamed **Cerdic Ferry**) took up the Europort service with two sailings a day.

Meanwhile, at Cairnryan, the **Free Enterprise IV** sailed South on 10th July 1986, on the arrival of the **Ionic Ferry** (ex **Dragon**) following her month's refit at Glasgow after leaving Portsmouth. The cabins and passenger areas situated aft on the **Ionic Ferry** were removed during her refit to enable her top deck area at the stern to be used for the carriage of high-sided vehicles. The **Ionic Ferry**, with her operating partner

The **Hellas** and **Syria** were chartered by Townsend Thoresen during the Falklands War in 1982 to maintain the Europort link, following the departure of the **Nordic Ferry** and **Baltic Ferry** to the South Atlantic. (Author's collection)

*Following the reorganisation of the Townsend Thoresen fleet for 1986, the **Ionic Ferry** (ex. **Dragon**) was transferred from Portsmouth to Larne. The former P&O Normandy Ferries vessel makes a pleasant scene at Larne during her first year on the link. (Larne P.R. Archives)*

*The **Viking Viscount** leaves Felixstowe for Zeebrugge on her morning sailing, whilst the **Nordic Ferry** can be seen loading for Europort. (Bruce Monaghan)*

Conversion of Baltic Ferry & Nordic Ferry

Two views of the **Nordic Ferry** undergoing conversion in Holland, prior to her entry into the Zeebrugge service in 1986 with her sister the **Baltic Ferry**. (P&O European Ferries)

The **Baltic Ferry** and the **Nordic Ferry** in the final stages of conversion at Rotterdam in 1986. The **Koningin Beatrix** can be seen in the background in the final stages of fitting-out for service. (P&O European Ferries)

The Atlantic Bar and Reception Area on the **Nordic Ferry**. (P&O European Ferries)

*The **Dragon** was built for P&O Normandy Ferries in 1965 for their Southampton - Le Havre service. The **Dragon** is captured here in P&O Ferries' livery and prior to her cabins being removed from the aft passenger accommodation. (Foto Flite 18038)*

*During 1987 the **Viking Trader** was transferred from Portsmouth to cover for the overhaul periods at Felixstowe and Larne. The "Trader" is seen here swinging off the berth at Larne. (Author's collection)*

the **Europic Ferry** then settled down into a regular pattern of sailings on the link.

The former Felixstowe "Super Vikings" quickly established themselves on the Portsmouth - Cherbourg link.

Following the take-over of European Ferries Group by the P&O Group on 5th December 1986, operations at Felixstowe and Larne have remained very much the same. The operating name of the European Ferries Group, Townsend Thoresen, disappeared on 21st October 1987, as part of a reorganisation of the Company, and the new P&O European Ferries Group was launched. The livery

and colours of the vessels were changed during the Winter of 1988 to dark blue hulls, with the P&O houseflag on the funnels.

The Larne - Cairnryan service is currently operated by the **Ionic Ferry** and **Europic Ferry**. Major changes must soon be on the cards, in the light of increased competition on the Irish Sea.

At Felixstowe, the **Nordic Ferry** and **Baltic Ferry** continue to cover the Zeebrugge route. The established link to Holland remains in the hands of the **Doric Ferry** and the **Cerdic Ferry** each operating two sailings a day.

*The **Ionic Ferry** on passage to Larne, shortly after her refit and conversion for the Ulster service. (Author's collection)*

*The **Nordic Ferry** on passage to Zeebrugge following her conversion to a passenger vessel. (Foto Flite 81108)*

*After 23 years in service, the **Europic Ferry** arrives at Larne from Scotland. (Miles Cowsill)*

NINE

A.S.N. at War

The A.S.N. Fleet has been involved in two international incidents since the Second World War. In the first part of this chapter Captain W. Close describes A.S.N.'s involvement in the Suez Crisis. Captain E. Harrison of the **Baltic Ferry** then relates his vessel's operations in the Falklands War.

THE SUEZ CANAL CRISIS

By early 1956 four vessels were based at Preston for the Northern Ireland service of A.S.N.: **Empire Cedric**, **Empire Doric**, **Empire Gaelic**, **Empire Cymric** and the S.S. **Empire Nordic** which had been recently acquired in anticipation of opening a Preston - Dublin service, but despite all efforts this was never to materialise. I was at that time Master of the **Empire Doric**.

In late July 1956 the Egyptian Government decided to nationalise the Suez Canal Company and take control of operating the Canal itself. Control of the Suez Canal had always been vital to Britain's trade and welfare. It was an extremely emotive issue, so it is not surprising that the British Government was determined to regain its influence, by armed action if necessary.

At Larne on 15th August, word arrived that all available LSTs were to be requisitioned forthwith for Government service. The ships were allowed to load the few pieces available on the quay and returned to Preston. No concessions were made to bring back vehicles and drivers left on the Irish side. In light of subsequent movements, the service could easily have operated for a further week.

Empire Cedric, **Empire Doric** and **Empire Gaelic** arrived in Birkenhead from Preston on 17th August. These three ships were unable to carry the heavier tanks then in service and it was proposed to stiffen the decks for this purpose. However, at that time a boilermakers' strike was in progress and plans were made to shore up the decks with timber. How this would have lasted in a seaway is a matter of conjecture. The plan was abandoned and **Empire Doric** was loaded

The **Empire Gaelic**, **Empire Doric** and the **Empire Cedric** moored in the Grand Harbour, Valetta, Malta with a Royal Navy LST. (S. Livingstone collection)

with motor transport and armoured personnel carriers, with about 140 men from the Grenadier Guards, with which we left Birkenhead at the end of August for Cowes Roads anchorage in company with several other requisitioned ships. I believe at that stage the plan was for a landing at Alexandria and a drive to Cairo. Although this was not stated there were charts and plans issued for that area.

A further period of inactivity then ensued, and life settled to a leisurely routine, the ship's motor lifeboat being used for trips ashore.

This period lasted for about three weeks when preparations for a different operation seemed to be afoot. **Empire Doric** was ordered to proceed to the Military Port of Marchwood. The contingent of Guards and their vehicles were discharged and transport, communications vehicles and men of the Royal Corps of Signals were embarked.

With these on board we sailed for Malta. It was a pleasant voyage out, arriving there early in October about the same time as the **Empire Gaelic** and **Empire Cedric**. All vehicles and troops were discharged and the three ships went to moorings in Valetta Harbour. Little then occurred apart from a practice loading in mid-October, until the end of the month.

About 30th October all three ships were again loaded with the vehicles and troops which had been brought from the U.K. They left Grand Harbour for an assembly anchorage in

The **Empire Cedric** moored in the Grand Harbour, Valetta, Malta prior to the Suez Crisis. (S. Livingstone collection)

Above: Army lorries loading on board the **Empire Doric** at Malta in October 1956. (Captain W. Close, Retired)

Right: A busy scene at Port Said in November 1956. The **Empire Cedric** can be seen discharging onto the beach. (Captain W. Close, Retired, collection)

Marsaxlokk Bay on the South side of the island. There a convoy conference was held ashore and shortly afterwards the ships left in convoy under sealed orders towards Port Said.

I remember there were about 15 to 20 ships in the convoy, a few RN LSTs, three A.S.N. LSTs, several merchant ships and various salvage craft. The ships were blacked out at night but the experience could not be compared with a war-time convoy. The use of radar was permitted for station keeping and radio silence was not enforced.

This convoy arrived off Port Said on the night of 6th/7th November. The main assault had already taken place, and the cease-fire was declared before any of the ships entered. The three LSTs of A.S.N. went to allocated berths in Port Said Harbour on the morning of 7th November, the **Empire Doric** berthing and discharging on the quay wall in the outer Harbour. I believe these were the first A.S.N. vessels to enter Port Said. There was no opposition and little danger involved, but several burning buildings and columns of black smoke created the classic invasion background.

After discharge **Empire Doric** sailed for Famagusta and returned to Port Said with further vehicles, supplies and personnel. The ship returned to Famagusta and made a trip to Tobruk with a few pieces of cargo, returning again to Cyprus. The ship then lay at anchor until mid-December when it was decided to dry-dock in Naples for overhaul and survey, affairs in the Canal Zone being apparently at a stalemate. Remaining in Naples until early January 1957, **Empire Doric** sailed for Malta. There troops and vehicles which had been evacuated from Port Said were loaded and the vessel sailed for the U.K., arriving in Tilbury about 18th January.

During the passage home severe weather was encountered in the Bay of Biscay, damaging the bow doors. After discharge the ship sailed to Liverpool for repairs. The vessel was handed back to the Ministry of Transport and towed to the Clyde. With the expected delivery of **Bardic Ferry** and recent acquisition of **Empire Cymric** and **Empire Nordic**, **Empire Doric** was considered surplus to requirements.

The Suez Canal operation originally was termed "Hannibal". This was later changed to "Operation Musketeer" which may have been when the plan was changed from Alexandria to Port Said.

The **Empire Gull** and **Empire Guillemot** pictured at Malta in 1958. (A. Morehew collection)

Captain W. Close, (Retired)
Larne

The Falklands War: Baltic Ferry And Her Part In Operation Corporate

In 1982, General Galtieri, President of Argentina, was having a little difficulty running the country, and decided the restless populace needed a diversion. For some years Argentina had been having talks with the British about the sovereignty of the Falkland Islands, 400 miles off the coast. Successive U.K. Governments had talked, talked, and prevaricated. It seemed like a ready-made solution to his problem and in early April the Argentine forces landed on the Islands, and unwittingly became part of the history of Atlantic Steam Navigation and Townsend Thoresen.

The British Government responded quickly, and decided to send a task force to recover the islands, though this was not as easy as it sounds because, in the years since the War, defence policy had slimmed the Navy down to sufficient only to support a NATO-type war in North West Europe. There was a serious

The **Baltic Ferry** was to form part of the Task Force in the Falklands War in 1982, with her sister the **Nordic Ferry**. The **Baltic Ferry** is seen here arriving at Felixstowe prior to service in the South Atlantic, with **Viking Viscount** loading for her morning sailing to Zeebrugge. (Bruce Monaghan)

shortage of transports to supply an invasion force 8000 miles away in the South Atlantic. The only answer was to get STUFT, in other words reinforce the Armed Forces with merchant Ships Taken Up From Trade. This in itself presented a problem as there was not a lot of choice left due to the massive decline of the Merchant Navy in the 1970s. After the **Canberra** and **Norland** had been requisitioned to carry troops, it seemed to me it would not be long before Their Lordships at the Admiralty would be looking for something suitable to carry their kit and vehicles. M.V. **Elk**, a ferry with similar features to our Felixstowe-based vessels, had already been taken up. Sure enough their eyes fell on the **Europic Ferry**, once an A.S.N. ship now operated by Thoresens at Southampton, and I sat at home on leave, having just completed my first month as a newly-promoted Master, wondering how far they would cast their net.

I was not disappointed. Captain Alan Young, my opposite number on the **Baltic Ferry**, called me to say that both the "Baltic" and **Nordic Ferry** had been taken up, and were proceeding to Portsmouth for a few modifications and to load arms and ammunition. Did I want to go? What did he mean? Did I want to go to Portsmouth, or did I want to go to the Falklands? Shortly after, Crew Manager Mike Hibbert 'phoned and left me in no doubt — "How would you like to go on a cruise in the South Atlantic?" I can't say I made my mind up in a flash, but suffice it to say I was given a few extra days at home before joining the **Baltic Ferry** at Southampton on 7th May 1982.

The ship was still loading cargo. Various tanks had been reconnected to the bunker system. A fresh water generator had been fitted, and a Re-fuelling at Sea (RAS) point rigged on the upper deck. The extensive open area ahead of the bridge had been strengthened, some obstructions cleared, and two helicopter landing pads marked out. Already it seemed this war was going to be heavily dependent on helicopters.

A lot of Naval communications and a satellite link had been fitted. There was a Royal Navy complement of 13 to operate this gear and act as helicopter handlers. Lt. Commander Ian Webb was in charge of them, and to act as my right-hand man. Inevitably the normal MN crew dubbed these ratings "Webb's Wonders".

On Sunday 9th May, the **Baltic Ferry** and **Nordic Ferry** sailed

from Southampton, with no other ships in company, but instructed to stay together "for the duration of the intended voyage". In all we had 162 souls on board, 43 MN crew, 14 RN and 105 Army personnel. The latter were small elements of many units, all of whom had some of their equipment on board, and included 4th Field Regiment Royal Artillery, 1st/7th Gurkhas, 10 Field Workshop Royal Engineers, 16th Field Ambulance RAMC, Royal Corps of Transport, 656 Squadron Army Air Corps, 81 Ordnance Company, and Scots Guards, Welsh Guards, and Royal Marines. A motley crew indeed.

Our cargo was equally varied - 3 Scout Helicopters, 45 Land Rovers, 15 motor cycles, 10 Snowtrack vehicles and three 105mm guns were included in the total of 1600 tons. There were 592 tons of stores of all sorts from tents to barbed wire, and petrol in jerry cans. There were also 400 tons of ammunition stowed on the lowest deck, which included 105mm ammunition (188 tons), small arms (40 tons), 84mm ammunition (126 tons) and the rest made up of rockets, missiles, mortar and phosphorous bombs, A nice little cocktail.

All this cargo was part of the equipment of the Fifth Infantry Brigade, the bulk of whose troops were to follow us in the **Queen Elizabeth 2**. We were given to understand that 5th Brigade would land after consolidation of the bridgehead established by the 3rd Brigade (Paras and Commandos) and effect recapture of the Islands. There was a vague idea that we would perhaps go to South Georgia, which had just been recaptured, and using the sheltered harbour there transfer our cargoes to the Royal Fleet Auxiliary transports.

As we headed South into warmer climes the troops checked and exercised with their equipment, including the 105mm guns. The helicopters practised deck landings and the crew were organised into action stations. This was practised twice daily and all these activities began to imbue in us a sense of impending excitement, tinged with danger. A brief stop at Freetown to refuel and we set off for Ascension Island, which was now an advanced base for all forces en route to the Falklands,

Between Freetown and Ascension we crossed the Equator and treated ourselves to an afternoon of fun and frolic as King Neptune dealt with those invading his domain for the first time.

Under orders to lay well off the Island, we spent most of the day loading a few tons of stores urgently needed further South, from a Chinook helicopter. We also took on board 20 RAF Harrier technicians. All our four-berth cabins were sleeping five, so they would now have to sleep on the cafeteria floor. It was 20th May - Ascension Day.

British troops landed on the Falklands the next day.

Of several new arts we had to practice, one of the hardest tasks was learning to darken ship. The two ships waltzed around one another several times looking for stray gleams of light. We all attended lectures on damage control, aircraft recognition and anything else thought to be useful. Our Third Engineer won a rifle-shooting competition beating all comers, much to the chagrin of the Guards and Gurkhas. We were told to sort cargo ready for exchange with the **QE2**. It looked as though South Georgia was "on".

*Captain Harrison on the bridge of the **Baltic Ferry** during an air raid in San Carlos Water in June 1982.*

The weather grew colder as we left the tropics and entered the South Atlantic autumn. The rendezvous with QE2 was cancelled. The "Nordic" and "Baltic" were given separate instructions - and different courses to steer. We were not to see our soul-mate for several days. Our instructions were to turn West towards the Falklands and commence zig-zag as an anti-submarine precaution. This day HMS **Coventry** was sunk by bombs and the **Atlantic Conveyor** hit by Exocet missile - I remembered her Captain, years ago when I was an apprentice in the Port Line, now missing along with eleven of her crew. Up to now the fear of danger had seemed more real than danger itself. Suddenly it was looming closer in our lives.

On 30th May, we entered the Total Exclusion Zone around the Islands, and the weather was cold and misty with fresh winds. We had all become avid listeners to the BBC World Service and were aware that the landings had been successful. Now we heard of the battle at Goose Green and it seemed that the outbreak had begun without waiting for the 5th Brigade to arrive. We were sent to an area 150 miles East of the Islands known as LOLA, the Logistics Loitering Area, to await orders. It seemed obvious now that we were going to go all the way in to the beach-head ourselves.

Next day we were called in to rendezvous with the Carrier Group between us and the Islands, and we passed the **Canberra**, **Norland** and **Europic Ferry** heading East as we hurried West to keep the appointment. The **Europic Ferry** had been my first temporary command two years before. She looked out of place in the cold dawn of 52 degrees South latitude.

The seas were running high when we met HMS **Hermes** and **Invincible** and a gaggle of frigates and RFA support vessels. Helicopters hopped between the ships and soon we

were receiving and offloading an assortment of stores in what were borderline conditions for deck landings. The deck was windswept and rainswept, and the ship rolled sickeningly most of the time. The deck party were exhausted as darkness fell, and we broke away to the West to pick up an escort. At last we had been ordered in to San Carlos.

On 1st June it was our personal D-Day. In company with the **Atlantic Causeway** and RFA **Blue Rover**, with HMS **Brilliant** as escort, we headed round the North side of East Falkland. HMS **Minerva** took over as we passed into the Sound, and HMS **Yarmouth** joined as rearguard. We found our allocated anchorage in San Carlos Water in total darkness and with minimum use of radar. Ramp down and cargo discharge commenced immediately. The Scouts flew off at the first hint of dawn. Daylight revealed about 12 vessels in the anchorage mostly huddled to one side against the hills. The wreck of the sunken HMS **Antelope** protruded through the surface near Red Beach, at Ajax Bay. During the day there were three air raid alerts but nothing was seen. In the daylight the air was full of helicopters of all sorts, and we unloaded from top deck to them, and to Mexeflotes at the stern ramp. That night we moved to the head of the bay to let other transports in nearer the beach landing areas.

The next day was foggy and we were duly grateful. A foggy day keeps the bombers away. We returned to the beachheads and continued unloading though the pace was slower as there were more transports but only so many Mexeflotes. When the first air raid warnings were given we stopped work and closed the ramps, but as time went by and nothing materialised we became blasé and kept on working, though everyone stayed at action stations. We needed to top up our fuel reserves from RFA **Tidespring** at the next anchorage. He wasn't very keen to accommodate us. We told him we had some fuel hoses on board for him, but the helicopters were busy elsewhere. He had a sudden change of mind and in a little while we were alongside him and the oil was flowing one way and his spare hoses were going the other.

That night we were ordered to leave San Carlos and return to lonely LOLA. Only half our cargo was ashore, but we didn't have the whole picture. Some of the landing ships were backloading for landings at Bluff Cove and Teal Inlet, so we couldn't be dealt with and we would be safer at sea. I believed it, as now we were reduced to a few rifles and one sub-machine gun for defence.

Three days in LOLA without immediate company and then we went back to San Carlos with the **Elk** and **Norland**. It was 7th June and seemed like the shortest, busiest week of my life. We anchored near HMS **Exeter**, and during the first Red Alert of the day he fired off two Seadart missiles and we watched the debris of the first fall on the surrounding hills. A rogue apparently. The second disappeared to the North and found

*HMS **Penelope** passing between the **Baltic Ferry** and the **Atlantic Causeway**. (Captain E. Harrison)*

*A Chinook helicopter operating from the **Baltic Ferry**.
(Captain E. Harrison)*

*The **Baltic Ferry** and the **Tor Caledonia** at Port Stanley.
(Captain E. Harrison)*

a target 30 miles away. The rest of the attackers apparently turned away. Unloading was slow due to lack of "Assets", the LCVs and one Mexeflote having gone to support the Teal and Bluff Cove landings. Helicopters were also thinner in the air as the Army moved their guns across the island.

Next day we were plagued with Red Alerts but no attacks until late afternoon when HMS **Plymouth** was hit by Skyhawks at the top of the Sound. She anchored under the protection of the Rapier missile sites now on the hills around San Carlos, and we watched the smoke pour from her. In an hour or so all seemed to be well, the smoke stopped and she regained her upright stance as the pumps dealt with the flooding. We remained at action stations most of the evening but further attacks were discouraged by Harriers now based just North of us at Port San Carlos.

This pattern continued for the next few days, though on 8 June there was, unusually, much helicopter activity after dark. The survivors of the Bluff Cove incident were being lifted into the field hospital at Ajax Bay. On the 10th we were pleased to see the **Nordic Ferry** arrive in the anchorage and to find that all was well with her. Later we took on board some POWs and left for sea under cover of darkness. Most of our cargo was now ashore; all we had left were "Defence Stores" - barbed wire and bricks, and about 10% of the ammunition.

We stooged about in TRALA, Tug Repair and Logistics Area (LOLA had been retired) for the next few days. The Argentine POWs were all kept under armed guard, and we expected to pass them on to a northbound RFA but apparently there wasn't one passing by. Meanwhile the advance to Port Stanley continued. The artillery flashes could be seen at night away to the West. We heard that HMS **Glamorgan** had suffered an Exocet hit but had survived. That sounded encouraging. On the 13th, we were ordered to meet the Carrier Battle Group again, and we spent the whole of a foggy day receiving medical supplies and other "goodies" from every ship that had any to spare, for onward delivery to San Carlos. In the afternoon we lent the POWs a short wave radio so they could listen to the World Cup football match. Belgium beat Argentina 1-0. "Not a good day for Argentina" said their senior Major. Some time in the small hours of the night, during the run-in, we passed the **Nordic Ferry** coming out, and we both had a bit of a scare as the escorting frigates, **Arrow** and **Penelope** declared a Red Alert. The **Penelope** let fly at something, but in the darkness nothing was seen and no attack developed.

In the morning we anchored again in San Carlos and got rid of the last of our ammunition. Everyone was delighted to see it go. During the rest of the day the medical stores went to Ajax Bay. There were rumours of a cease-fire as our troops

closed on Port Stanley. The weather was pretty cold and miserable with snow on the hills. A good incentive for any army, defending or attacking, to get it over and done with, one way or another.

On 15th June, the surrender was confirmed in the morning - it's all over. Our delight was immeasurable, and we all had silly grins on our faces. Our POW's were fairly philosophical about it when I broke the news to them, but the major shook my hand and said ruefully - "Not a good day for Argentina".

We remained in San Carlos for several days backloading some of the accumulated stores on the beaches now that they were not needed for battle. It was frustrating work as there were never enough Mexeflotes or LCVs allocated to us and everything came on in dribs and drabs. We played hostel to any of the troops ashore in tents and foxholes. If they could get out to us we gave them a hot meal, a shower, a few beers etc. to help them feel a bit more civilized. In due course our POW's went to the **Norland** who took them and thousands of others to Argentina. Meanwhile in San Carlos the most severe storm sprang up, and as we swung snugly at our anchor we thought of our colleagues aboard the **Nordic Ferry** out in it somewhere. We learned later they had had a very bad time and were driven almost to South Georgia before the storm passed over them.

Although the battle for the Islands was over the Argentine Government would say no more than that hostilities had ceased "de facto". Our masters therefore felt they could restart any time if the mainland forces decided to have another "go", so for the time being we continued to live in blackout conditions. For a month now we had been living with all windows permanently covered and if you worked indoors only the clock told you if it was night or day.

After nine days' frustration we were ordered to Fitzroy. I did not like the idea as the coast there was low-lying and featureless and the water shallow. We would have to find our way in, in the dark. As it happened we arrived there in a blinding rainstorm. We had hardly dropped anchor, with less than three feet of water under the keel, when we were told to move to Port Stanley. This we were glad to do and we arrived there in bright sunshine. Port William, the outer harbour, was full of ships including the **Intrepid**, **Fearless**, **Canberra**, **Norland** and **Europic Ferry**. Later we moved to the inner harbour of Port Stanley itself. The town seemed small and the iron roofs of the buildings gave it a shanty look. Even the cathedral roof was corrugated iron. I wasn't surprised the Argentinians didn't think it worth fighting over.

In a few days our fate was decided. The **Nordic Ferry** was to go home, via South Georgia, changing the garrison there. The **Baltic Ferry** was to remain in Port Stanley as a floating warehouse until better facilities were available on shore for all the garrison equipment arriving from the U.K. On 20th August Captain Roger Edwards and a relief crew arrived and we could go home. We had made good use of the intervening weeks on trips ashore, courtesy of the helicopter crews, and visited far-flung parts of the Islands, but the monotony of the treeless landscape, though beautiful in its own way, only nurtured the urge to get home. The **Baltic Ferry** remained until March 1983, leaving the vicinity of Stanley only once, on an errand to Fox Bay on West Falkland, by then under a third crew commanded by Captain Mike Metcalf.

Our crew travelled North to Ascension on the South Atlantic Ferry, the poor old **Norland**, also still in bondage to the Ministry of Defence. The trip was not a happy one. Conditions were not too good and the food was terrible. From Ascension we flew home courtesy of RAF Transport Command. At Brize Norton the A.S.N. Management laid on a great reception for us and our families, a rapturous welcome complete with brass band and champagne. It was good to be back.

On a personal note, I had been in the ferries for sixteen years, and had occasionally felt the urge to do another deep sea voyage like those of my earlier days. Somehow the urge had disappeared, but I am glad I went.

Captain E. Harrison
Baltic Ferry, Felixstowe

*Relatives of the crew welcome home the **Baltic Ferry** at Felixstowe. (Bruce Monaghan)*

TEN

Europic Ferry

THE LAST OF THE LINE

The **Europic Ferry** was ordered in April 1966 and launched on Tuesday 3rd October 1967, being specifically designed for the new service from Felixstowe to Europort. A.S.N. started using the Port of Felixstowe during July 1965, with the **Gaelic Ferry**. The new Suffolk port was so successful that the larger and faster **Europic Ferry** was ordered to increase sailings and establish Europort as the new Dutch terminal, in favour of Rotterdam.

The **Europic Ferry** was built by Swan Hunter at Wallsend-on-Tyne and was designed to operate at speeds of up to 18 knots in a loaded condition which, together with her fast turnarounds, would enable the vessel to make at least six voyages a week to the new terminal of Europort.

Like the earlier ships of this class, the **Europic Ferry** was designed with a virtually unobstructed garage deck space, with access through a large stern door. Her vehicle deck was designed with a lower car deck area abaft her engine room, like the **Gaelic Ferry,** for the export of cars and trailers. Access to this lower car deck was via a hydraulic ramp on the main deck.

The original combined garage space of the **Europic Ferry** allowed almost 100 road vehicles or 10-metre trailers to be carried. In the original design, containers could be stowed on the clear upper deck. Careful note was taken at the design stage of the vessel of the growing container trade between the UK and the Continent. The management of A.S.N. at the time foresaw a probable levelling-off of the demand for roll-on/roll-off traffic and therefore the **Europic Ferry** was built on the basis of an eventual conversion to a full container ship had the need arisen. In the event, ro-ro traffic was to grow faster than container traffic, and her upper deck was later to be utilised for high-sided vehicles and passenger cars instead of containers.

The **Europic Ferry**, like her earlier sisters, was built to the requirements of the Ministry of Defence, in case the vessel had to be called up for war. In the event, she was to play an important role in the Falklands War, some 14 years after entering service.

The launch of the Europic Ferry on 3rd October 1967. (Author's collection)

EUROPIC FERRY	
Gross tons	4,190
Net	1,499
Deadweight	2,784
Length (o.a)	137.26m
Breadth (Extr.)	21.06m
Draught (max)	4.57m
Passengers	160
Vehicles (max)	272 cars or 40 lorries
Builders	Swan Hunter, Wallsend, UK
Yard No.	2025
Launch	3rd October 1967
Entered service	18 January 1968
Engines	Two 6,700 bhp Pielstick IB
Speed (knots)	16
Call Sign	GYCD
Present route (1990/91)	Larne - Cairnryan

*The **Europic Ferry** is slowly manoeuvred to her fitting-out basin following her launch. The **Antrim Princess** can be seen in the background fitting-out at Swan Hunter's Yard. (Author's collection)*

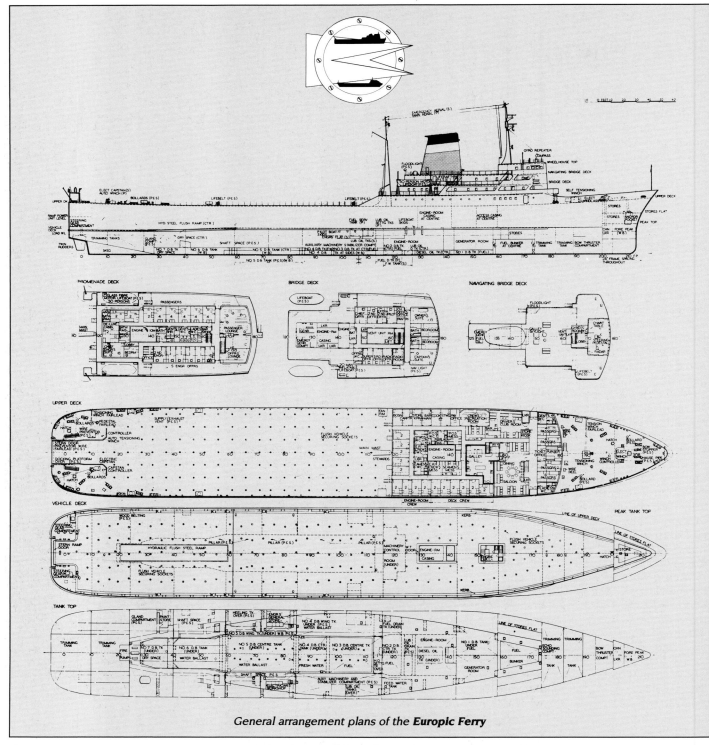

General arrangement plans of the **Europic Ferry**

The **Gaelic Ferry** and the **Europic Ferry** pictured at Felixstowe in May 1971. (Ambrose Greenway)

Captain's Suite. (Author's collection)

The **Europic Ferry** boasted an Owners' Suite and Cabin, for the use of the Directors and special V.I.P.s travelling with the Company. (Author's collection)

The **Europic Ferry** originally could accommodate 44 passengers in her very well-appointed two and three-berth cabins, including an owners' cabin suite. Her passenger certificate was increased in 1980 to 60 passengers. Four years later when she entered service between Larne and Cairnryan, her certificate was increased to 160 by removing some cabins on the main passenger deck.

The amenities and standard of accommodation on board the **Europic Ferry** were equal in many ways to those of deep sea vessels. The "Europic" was the last of the line and was not only to be the fastest and largest ship ever to be built for A.S.N., but also the best appointed when she entered service.

One of the most important differences between the **Europic Ferry** and the earlier ships of the series was the selection of Pielstick-type machinery for the main propulsion. The **Europic Ferry** was fitted with two Lindholmen-built 16 PC2V units, each rated at 6,780 bhp. A separate auxiliary compartment was built forward of the main engine room to house four W.H. Allen 470 kW diesel engine generators. The **Europic Ferry** like her earlier sisters was built with the benefit of stabilisers for the comfort of her passengers and for the safety of goods stowed on board.

A unique feature of the **Europic Ferry** was the sound-proofed machinery control station in the engine room, which was to provide a pleasant environment for those working in the engineering department of the vessel.

Another feature of the **Europic Ferry** was the use of teak decks. This typified at the time the Company's attitude to their new ship as a whole; proven and time-tested equipment was employed where there was no need for change, while at the same time no expense was spared to secure a well-presented ship at the end of the day.

The **Europic Ferry** entered service at Felixstowe on 18th January 1968 on the Company's new Europort link, following a short visit to Tilbury, which A.S.N. closed some nine months later. The "Europic" was to become the mainstay of the Dutch and the Belgian services for the next decade, with her operating partners the **Gaelic Ferry** and the **Cerdic Ferry**.

During 1981, the **Europic Ferry** was transferred from Felixstowe to Southampton to replace the **Viking IV** on the Le Havre freight run. Her place at Felixstowe was taken by the chartered Stena-built ships **Stena Transporter** and **Merzario Hispania**, later to be renamed **Baltic Ferry** and **Nordic Ferry**.

The **Europic Ferry's** main claim to fame came during the Falklands War of 1982, when she was one of a number of short-sea vessels called up for active service.

The **Europic Ferry** was formally requisitioned on 19th April 1982, as a transport for 3 Commando Brigade. At

Dining Saloon. (Author's collection)

Passengers' Lounge and Bar. (Author's collection)

Cheering crowds greet the **Europic Ferry** at Southampton following her return from the Falklands War. (Author's collection)

The **Europic Ferry** makes an impressive sight in dry-dock during annual overhaul. (Larne P.R. Archives)

The **Europic Ferry** swings off the berth at Larne in June 1989. (Miles Cowsill)

Southampton the vessel was converted for use as a military ship; her modifications included the provision of RAS (Replenishment at Sea) equipment, salt water evaporator (to provide additional fresh water) with the necessary alterations to the ship's tanks, and fitting of a military radio station in the bridge deck pantry, as the ship's commercial radio office was not to be used. Provision of a special helicopter deck was not necessary on the **Europic Ferry**, as her long clear after deck was ideal for the purpose. Passenger accommodation and mess rooms were fitted with additional bunks and became a home to 75 men mainly from '2 Para' and their associated units.

The cargo for "Europic's" voyage to the South Atlantic included Scout Helicopters from 656 Squadron, Army Air Corps, vehicles, military stores and a large consignment of ammunition.

A 13-man Royal Navy party was embarked to run the communications and assist in all the aspects of the ship's new role prior to her sailing from Southampton on 22nd April for the war zone, under the command of Captain Chris Clarke. Some three days later, the "Europic" joined the **Atlantic Conveyor** off Plymouth.

The **Europic Ferry** was to make a valuable contribution in the Task Force operations and returned from the Falklands on 17th July 1982, looking a very different ship, from that which left in April. Her bright orange Townsend Thoresen livery had been daubed with grey in order to make her less conspicuous to the Argentine bombers. Following an extensive refit at Avonmouth, the Falklands hero entered service once again on 26th August on the Le Havre run.

The **Europic Ferry's** place on the Southampton - Le Havre freight run was taken by the **Gaelic Ferry** whilst she was in the Falklands.

The engine control room in the **Europic Ferry**. She was the only A.S.N. ship to be fitted with such an area. (John Hendy)

Some four months later, after the Falklands War, she was back in service at Felixstowe, following the loss of the **European Gateway**.

During March 1983, the **Europic Ferry** was transferred to the Larne - Cairnryan service, initially as a temporary replacement for the **Free Enterprise IV** which was required elsewhere in the fleet, and subsequently as a replacement for the **Gaelic Ferry**.

Following her transfer to the Northern service, the **Europic Ferry** quickly established herself as a worthwhile new addition to the operations between Scotland and Ireland. Modifications were carried out internally to the vessel in 1984 to increase her passenger certificate.

Following re-organisation of the fleet in 1986, the **Europic Ferry** was joined by the **Ionic Ferry** (ex **Dragon**) on the

*The author and Captain Willie McLellan on the starboard bridge wing of the **Europic Ferry** in July 1990. (John Hendy)*

Larne - Cairnryan route. The 17-year-old **Free Enterprise IV** was then transferred back to Dover to maintain the Boulogne service with her near sister **Free Enterprise V**.

The **Europic Ferry** currently maintains the Larne - Cairnryan service with the **Ionic Ferry** under the command of her four masters, Captain Edwards, Captain Ledger, Captain Keough and Captain McLellan

The grand old lady of the fleet and last surviving A.S.N. built vessel remains as valuable as ever, especially for the transportation of high-sided cattle vehicles between Northern Ireland and Scotland. The **Europic Ferry** still retains that special air of 'The Transport Ferry Service', even after 23 years under the management of three different companies during her distinguished career.

*The **Europic Ferry** inward to Southampton in September 1981. (Ambrose Greenway)*

ELEVEN

P&O European Ferries

The financial demise of European Ferries has been well documented elsewhere. It was therefore with some relief that on 14th December 1986 a bid was received from P&O and accepted by European Ferries' shareholders the following day. A.S.N. welcomed a new Chairman, P&O main Board director Mr. Peter Ford. Although P&O's acquisition of the ferry business was first marred by the tragedy of Zeebrugge, there is no doubt that to compete in this business today it is necessary to enjoy the resources of such an internationally successful and well-respected group.

Ten months after the takeover, on 21st October 1987, the trading name Townsend Thoresen was replaced by P&O European Ferries, and the former A.S.N. Company was renamed P&O European Ferries (Felixstowe) Ltd. Overnight a massive operation was carried out; signs, uniforms, stationery and vehicles all appeared the following day proudly bearing the P&O flag and livery to announce the transformation. The renamed A.S.N. Company, P&O European Ferries (Felixstowe) Ltd., took its place amongst the ranks of other famous companies which stretch to the four corners of the globe.

In the Spring of 1989, after over 40 years' service covering nearly the entire period of this book, Mr. Sidney Livingstone retired as Managing Director and was succeeded by Mr. John Palmer. 1989 was a record year for the Company for both freight and tourist carryings, fulfilling the P&O objective that each member company must compete effectively and profitably to secure their own future.

This book has faithfully recorded the history of the Atlantic Steam Navigation Company and, although the past should be remembered it is equally, if not more, important to look forward. Today, P&O European Ferries (Felixstowe) Ltd. and their employees, whether on board one of the fleet of six ships or ashore at Felixstowe, Europort, Larne or Cairnryan, have the benefit of a proud heritage and an exciting future.

*An impressive view of the **Nordic Ferry** on passage to Zeebrugge. (Foto Flite 71639)*

*The **Cerdic Ferry** outward bound for Europort sporting the new P&O European Ferries' livery in 1988. (P&O European Ferries)*

A.S.N. Scrapbook

The **Ionic Ferry** was sold by Townsend Thoresen in 1976 to the Swiss owned company, Neptunia Line. The former A.S.N. ship was renamed **Kamasin** and was later named **Tamerlane**. The Denny-built vessel is pictured here in 1987 as the **Tamerlane** laid-up in the Mediterranean. (Steffen Weirauch)

The **Bardic Ferry** was sold to the same owners as the 'Ionic' during 1976. The first purpose-built ship for A.S.N. was renamed **Nasim II** by her new owners for service in the Mediterranean. The former Preston-based vessel is seen here at the breakers in Turkey. (John Hendy collection)

The **Cerdic Ferry** and **Doric Ferry** were sold by European Ferries during 1981, after 20 years faithful service on the Irish Sea and North Sea, to Compania Armadora de Sudamerica. The former A.S.N. ships were renamed **Atlas I** (ex **Cerdic Ferry** — pictured here) and **Atlas II** (ex **Doric Ferry**) and they commenced their Greek career in service between Patras, Igoumenitsa and Brindisi. The former 'Cerdic' is currently named **Sifnos** and is in the ownership of Ventouris Line. Meanwhile the former 'Doric' is currently trading as the **Capetan Alexandros** under the management of Cycladic Lines. (Steffen Weirauch)

The **Free Enterprise III** was to make a powerful impact on the Larne — Cairnryan route in 1974 under A.S.N. management, as the company's first drive-through vessel on the link. The Townsend ship was sold in August 1984 to Maltese owners. She was subsequently sold again the same year to the Isle of Man Steam Packet Co. Ltd. After only one season on the Irish Sea she was sold again for use as a pilgrim ship in the Red Sea as **Al Fahad**. In this picture, the former Dover-based ship is seen leaving Douglas as the **Mona's Isle**, during her brief association with the Isle of Man. (Richard Danielson)

TOWNSEND THORESEN TT

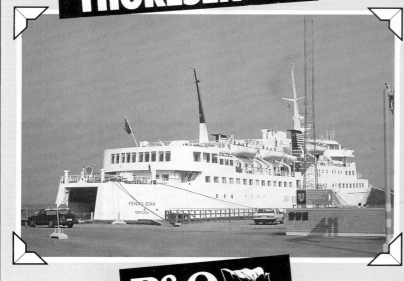

P&O European Ferries

*Above left: The **Viking II** which opened the Felixstowe - Zeebrugge service in October 1974, was sold four years later to Sealink, to open their new link to the Channel Islands from Portsmouth. The former Thoresen ship was renamed **Earl William** and was to have a colourful career with Sealink until June 1990. The **Earl William** is pictured here, leaving Dun Laoghaire for Liverpool in July 1988. (Miles Cowsill)*

*Above: Following **Free Enterprise IV** being transferred back to the English Channel in 1986, the former Larne-based vessel was to remain in the fleet for a further three years. She was sold to GT-Link and renamed **Falster Link** for her new role in the Baltic. (Tim Parsons)*

*Left: The **Viking III** was sold during 1981 to Da-No Line and renamed **Terje Vigen**. The vessel, which opened the passenger link between Felixstowe - Europort under A.S.N. management, currently is owned by Vaasanlaivat and operates as the **Fenno Express**. (Hans Beijar)*

*Below: The **Viking Voyager** and the **Viking Viscount** were transferred to the Portsmouth — Cherbourg link in 1986, as part of a reorganisation of the fleet. In 1989, the former Felixstowe 'Super Vikings' were renamed **Pride of Cherbourg** (ex **Viking Voyager**) and **Pride of Winchester** (ex **Viking Viscount**). The **Pride of Winchester** is seen here arriving at Cherbourg. (Miles Cowsill)*

A.S.N., Townsend Thoresen and P&O European Ferries Fleet List

	BUILDERS	YEAR/GROSS TONNAGE	SERVICE PERIOD	NOTES
Empire Baltic	Canadian, Vickers Ltd., Montreal	1945/4,157	1946—62	Broken up Spezia
Empire Cedric	Yarrows Ltd., Esquimault	1945/4,291	1946—59	Broken up Ghent
Empire Celtic	Davie Shipbuilding & Repairing Co. Ltd., Lauzon, Canada	1945/4,291	1946—60	Broken up Spezia
Empire Cymric	Harland & Wolff Ltd., Belfast	1945/4,291	1955—62	Broken up Faslane
Empire Doric	Harland & Wolff Ltd., Govan	1945/4,291	1948—60	Broken up Glasgow
Empire Gaelic	Davie Shipbuilding & Repairing Co. Ltd., Lauzon, Canada	1945/4,291	1948—60	Broken up Belgium
Empire Nordic	Blyth Dry Dock & Shipbuilding Co. Ltd.	1945/4,295	1955—66	Broken up in the Far East
Baltic Ferry (I)	American Bridge Co., Ambridge, U.S.A.	1943/1,909	1966—67	Sold 1972
Celtic Ferry	Newport News Shipbuilding, Virginia, U.S.A.	1944/5,556	1967—72	Sold 1973
Bardic Ferry	Wm. Denny & Bros. Ltd., Dumbarton	1957/2,550	1957—76	Sold 1976. Renamed: **Nasim II**
Ionic Ferry	Wm. Denny & Bros. Ltd., Dumbarton	1958/2,548	1958—76	Sold 1976. Renamed: **Kamasin/ Tamerlane**
Cerdic Ferry (I)	Ailsa Shipbuilding Co. Ltd., Troon	1961/2,563	1961—81	Sold 1981. Renamed: **Atlas I/ Sifnos**
Doric Ferry (I)	Ailsa Shipbuilding Co. Ltd., Troon	1962/2,573	1962—81	Sold 1981. Renamed: **Atlas II/ Captain Alexandros**
Gaelic Ferry	Swan Hunter & Wigham Richardson Ltd., Tyneside	1963/3,316*	1964—85	Sold 1987 for scrap
Europic Ferry	Swan Hunter (Shipbuilders) Ltd., Wallsend	1967/4,190	1968	Still in service. Larne - Cairnryan
Free Enterprise I	Werf Gusto, Schiedam, Holland	1962/2,606	1975	Larne - Cairnryan. Sold 1980. Renamed: **Kimolos**
Free Enterprise III	Werf Gusto, Schiedam, Holland	1966/4,567	1974	Larne - Cairnryan. Sold 1984. Renamed: **Tamira/Mona's Isle/Al Fahad**
Free Enterprise IV	Werf Gusto, Schiedam, Holland	1969/5,050	1976—86	Larne - Cairnryan. Sold 1988. Renamed: **Falster Link**
Viking II	Kaldnes M/VA/S Tonsberg, Norway	1964/3,670	1974—76	Felixstowe - Zeebrugge. Sold 1976. Renamed: **Earl William**
Viking III	Orenstein-Koppel und Lübecker Masch A/G, W. Germany	1965/3,824	1978—79	Felixstowe - Europort. Sold 1982. Renamed: **Terje Vigen/ Scandinavia/Fenno Express**
Viking Valiant	Aalborg Vaerft A/S, Aalborg, Denmark	1975/6,387	1975—76	Felixstowe - Zeebrugge. Transferred to Southampton 1976
Viking Voyager	Aalborg Vaerft A/S, Aalborg, Denmark	1976/6,387	1976—86	Felixstowe - Zeebrugge. Transferred to Portsmouth 1986
Viking Viscount	Aalborg Vaerft A/S, Aalborg, Denmark	1976/6,387	1976—86	Felixstowe - Zeebrugge. Transferred to Portsmouth 1986
European Gateway	Schichau Unterweser AG, Bremerhaven	1975/4,263*	1975—82	Felixstowe. Sold 1983. Renamed: **Flavia/Travenmunde Link**
Baltic Ferry (II)	Hyundai Heavy Industries, S. Korea	1978/18,732*	1981	Felixstowe - Europort & Zeebrugge.
Nordic Ferry	Hyundai Heavy Industries, S. Korea	1978/18,732*	1980	Felixstowe - Europort & Zeebrugge.
Ionic Ferry (II)	Dubigeon-Normandie, Nantes, France	1967/5,777	1986	Larne - Cairnryan
Cerdic Ferry (II)	Hyundai Heavy Industries, S. Korea	1978/8,579	1986	Felixstowe - Europort
Doric Ferry (II)	Hyundai Heavy Industries, S. Korea	1977/8,579	1986	Felixstowe - Europort

*After stretching/conversion

A.S.N. Fleet List Managed on Behalf of The Ministry of Defence in the Mediterranean & Far East

Frederick Clover Snowden Smith Charles MacLeod Evan Gibb Reginald Kerr Humphrey Gale Maxwell Brander
Empire Gull Empire Guillemot Empire Tern Empire Skua Empire Petrel Empire Puffin Empire Kittiwake Empire Shearwater
Empire Fulmar Empire Grebe Empire Gannet Empire Curlew

Coastal Container Fleet — See Chapter 7

THE AUTHOR

Miles Cowsill was born in 1955 and spent his early childhood in Barry, South Wales before moving to Kent in 1962. Early family motoring holidays on the Continent introduced him to the delights of the small Townsend car ferry **Free Enterprise** and there began a lifelong interest in this specialist type of ship.

In 1979 Miles Cowsill moved to Pembrokeshire where he started his association with his friend and Ferry Publications Partner, John Hendy, by becoming the Welsh correspondent for John's monthly article in "Sea Breezes" magazine.

Married with a small son, Miles devotes much of his spare time to writing, photography and with his wife Linda, to running the Ferry Publications office. Recent solo titles have included the history of Brittany Ferries, British Channel Island Ferries and Sealink's Fishguard - Rosslare route.

This title has been the most demanding book so far for Miles Cowsill, dealing as it does with the history of the Company whose story has never before been explored. *J.F.H.*

FERRY PUBLICATIONS

Ferry Publications was formed in 1988 by Miles Cowsill and John Hendy who had joined together to write and publish their highly successful Townsend Thoresen Years. Since then they have produced a continuous stream of titles which have covered most areas of the North Sea, English Channel and Irish Sea.

Disenchantment with writing for other magazines led the Partners to launch their own quarterly journal, "British Ferry Scene" in the Summer of 1989. Now a firmly established favourite, the magazine has quickly gained praise from both the enthusiast fraternity and the ferry industry alike.

Richard Danielson joined the team later in 1989, adding his considerable expertise to that of the founder Partners who today are the leaders in this fascinating and highly specialised field.

For further information and details on current titles of Ferry Publications, please write to: 12 Millfields Close, Pentlepoir, Kilgetty, Dyfed SA68 0SA. *J.F.H.*

FOTO FLITE

Ferry Publications is proud to be associated with Britain's leading marine aerial photographers. Foto Flite pride themselves on offering a very personal service to their customers requesting photographs from their archives of 500,000 negatives of ships which have plied around our shores since 1947. Most of the outstanding aerial photographs in this book have been kindly provided by Foto Flite; these and many other historical pictures of ships of different shapes and sizes can be purchased from the company. For further details and price list, contact: Foto Flite, Littlestone Road, New Romney, Kent TN28 8LW, England.
(Tel: 0679 64891, Telex: 96303)

I would like to express my gratitude and thanks to all the staff at Foto Flite, especially Philip Neumann, Director and Nigel Scutt for all their assistance with the publication.

ACKNOWLEDGEMENTS

I am grateful for the assistance of all those who have kindly contributed to this publication.

Firstly I would like to thank John Palmer, Managing Director of P&O European Ferries (Felixstowe), for writing the Foreword to the book and also for following its progress with interest and enthusiasm.

I would like to thank Spencer Smith, Passenger Marketing Manager, Felixstowe and Dennis Grattan, Public Relations Executive, Larne for all their assistance with the publication.

During the preparation of the book, I have received a tremendous amount of archive material from former A.S.N.

*Bridge Deck - **Europic Ferry**. (Miles Cowsill)*

staff. I regret that I am unable to thank all personally, however, your assistance and support has been much appreciated.

I should also like to thank Michael Bustard and Captain W. Close (Retired), for their contributions and for advising me on the early history of the Company. My thanks also go to Sid Livingstone, Captain Harrison, Hugh P. Ghee and Bernard McCall for their relevant chapters.

I am indebted to my good friend and partner in Ferry Publications John Hendy for assisting and advising with the publication.

Linda, my wife, should also receive a word of thanks for her assistance and support.

I would also like to thank all the staff at Haven Colourprint for their assistance with the production of the book.

Finally I would like to express my gratitude to David and Dorothy Parsons for reading and checking the proofs.

The following are also thanked for photographs and information:- Geoffrey Breeze, Klas Brogren, Paul Clegg, Richard Danielson (Ferry Publications), Captain H.T. Green (Retired), Ambrose Greenway, J. Hartill, Peter Inpijin, H. Irwin, Andy Jones, Ken Kane, Mike Louagie, Rodney MacKenna, Captain W. McLellan, Bruce Monaghan, A. Morehen, Tim Parsons, Nick Robins and Steffen Weirauch.

BIBLIOGRAPHY

British Nationalised Shipping — W. Paul Clegg & John S. Styring
The Short Sea Route — Fraser G. MacHaffie
The Townsend Thoresen Years — Miles Cowsill & John Hendy
The Viking Saga — Miles Cowsill & John Hendy